Philosophical Dialogues
on the Christian Faith

Philosophical Dialogues on the Christian Faith

Discussions on the Arguments, Evidence, and Truth of Christianity

STEVE WEST

PUBLISHERS
Eugene, Oregon

PHILOSOPHICAL DIALOGUES ON THE CHRISTIAN FAITH
Discussions on the Arguments, Evidence, and Truth of Christianity

Copyright © 2007 Steve West. All rights reserved. Except for brief quotations in critical publications or reviews, no part of this book may be reproduced in any manner without prior written permission from the publisher. Write: Permissions, Wipf & Stock, 199 W. 8th Ave., Eugene, OR 97401.

ISBN 13: 978-1-55635-142-6

Manufactured in the U.S.A.

To my wife Heather,
You're just too good to be true.

Contents

Acknowledgments / ix

Preface / xi

1
The Cosmological Argument / 1

2
The Teleological Argument / 15

3
Why God Does Not Exist / 31

4
Evil, the World, and God / 43

5
Rev. Laidler's Lecture / 59

6
Truth and the Resurrection / 71

7
Epistemology and Facts / 85

Bibliography / 99

Acknowledgments

Madoc Baptist Church, for letting me be part of you.

Mom and Dad, for being worthy of emulation. You make me proud.

Doug and Eleanor, for your acceptance and encouragement.

Andy and Loni, for your passion for the Gospel, both well presented and well defended.

Craig and Janet, for your commitment to truth and to each other. Craig, you are one of the most naturally inquisitive philosophers I have ever met.

Michael, Mark, and Jordan, for the numerous debates and conversations over the years. Your ability to explore logical modes through the semantics of possible worlds is breathtaking. My favorite such possible world is still, of course, 15-9.

Les, Laurie, and family, for being family in two different ways, neither of which was through genetics or marriage.

Heather and Charlotte, for more than I can say. You are great gifts of grace, and have provided me with more happiness, joy and love than any man deserves. Being a husband and a father has made me richer than I ever thought I could possibly be.

To all philosophers and apologists, for allowing me to profit from your scholarship, and to raid your resources for this book. You have shaped my thinking more than I can say.

Preface

This book is primarily designed to serve in one of two ways. The first way is as a supplement for those who have some background in studying the issues in philosophy concerning religion and the existence of God. Many beginning students find reading even "introductory" books on philosophy or apologetics hard going. It is hoped that this book will help to clarify the drift of some arguments the reader has already encountered. A second way this book can be used is an introduction to the subject matter. If this is the reader's first encounter with these philosophical arguments, it is hoped that this book will provide a stimulus to further study on the topics addressed.

Instead of heavy prose, the style of this book is that of a philosophical dialogue. The dialogue format has a long history in philosophy, and many readers have found it to be quite helpful. This book is written as a conversation in the hopes that it will lead to real life conversations and dialogues. Admittedly, some of the dialogue may seem stilted or somewhat unnatural. In real life, the conversations written here could have developed in dozens of different ways. Yet I do think that the direction of the conversation is at least plausible, for those with an open mind. Again, the various arguments could be substantiated and defended (and objected against) in much greater detail. Let me encourage the reader to do further study and research after reading this book. Just because an argument is not used or mentioned in these pages does not mean that it doesn't exist, or that it is not worthy of consideration!

One of the unique features of this book is that it presents the gospel message of Jesus Christ in the context of philosophical investigation and historical study. This is because, as one of the characters notes, it is possible to argue about whether or not Jesus was raised from the dead without understanding why that event is so important in Christian theology. To abstract the historical account of Jesus Christ's resurrection from its theological context is sure to generate a great misunderstanding of the Christian faith. Even if the reader denies that the resurrection actually happened, the reader should at least understand the importance of the resurrection for the Christian worldview. In order to really be resurrected, one first needs to be dead. Why did Jesus die? Understanding the answer to that question is absolutely necessary for understanding the central message of the Christian faith.

There is a subtle distinction in this book between philosophy and Christian apologetics. While my purpose is apologetic, the expressed purpose of Ron and Jay is not apologetic. They are not engaging in dialogue to defend the Christian faith: they are engaging in dialogue to philosophically investigate whether or not God exists. If I had cast one of the two characters as a Christian who was dialoguing with an individual representing a different worldview, the speeches and conversations would have been constructed in different ways. So there are two layers of purpose in this book: The first level order of my intention, and the second level order of the intention of the characters. If both of these orders had been collapsed into one (that is, if one of the characters was actually personally engaging in apologetics), the shape and flow of this book would be different.

The premise of this book is that two characters named Ron and Jay have decided to study arguments about the existence of God, and then get together to discuss their thoughts. Neither is an expert in any field, but they are both sincerely interested in their investigations. What they find, and the conversations they have, makes up the subject matter of this book.

One note should be made about the use of resources in this book. In most conversations, we do not take the time to provide footnotes. I have not used footnotes in the book because I thought it would be distracting to the flow of the dialogue. Also, hardly any of the arguments are particular to just one person. When one person is overwhelmingly influential in a given argument, their name has sometimes been incorporated directly into the text. Consulting the bibliography at the end of this volume will reveal the sources most heavily used. The bibliography does not, however, contain the numerous journal articles, theses, and dissertations that should be studied for deeper understanding of these issues. The basic arguments in the dialogues can all be found in the various books cited in the bibliography. Multiplying the citation of journal articles did not seem necessary.

I think that the genre of philosophical dialogue is a good fit for today's learner. This book goes out with the hope that another philosopher—one with more sensitivity to drama and literature—will produce a "classic" work in religious philosophy which will stand with Hume's Dialogues for centuries to come. Excellence in research, when combined with excellence in presentation, is a great combination. I make no claims to have achieved either, but I do hope that the reader profits from this book, and that it is soon improved upon by the work of another. Maybe that "another" is you.

I

The Cosmological Argument

RON. Hi Jay. How are you doing?

JAY. Fine. How about you?

RON. Fine, thanks. I studied as much about the cosmological argument as I could, and I have to admit that I was really interested in what I found. I had never even heard about this argument before, so I was shocked to find out that it's been discussed for thousands of years by some of the greatest philosophers who have ever lived. I don't think I understood everything that I read, but I think I got the general idea fairly accurately. It was really interesting stuff.

As far as I could understand it, the basic idea behind the cosmological argument is that you start with the way things are today, and then you move backwards using science or logic to figure out what had to happen for this state of affairs to end up the way that it is. It's like moving back links in a chain to find the beginning link, or counting down from ten to find the first number. If I want to know how I came to exist I look at my parents, but that just raises the question: How did they come to exist? To figure out why I exist today I need to start working backwards to find an ultimate answer.

Some of the arguments, particularly about contingent versus necessary beings, I found rather complex for right now, but some of the other strands of reasoning seemed to be much easier to grasp. I had heard about the Greeks' Unmoved Mover, but I never knew what that meant. Now I know that the Unmoved Mover was supposed to be the thing that got the ball rolling in our universe, so to speak. Nothing moved It, but It was supposed to have started everything else moving or changing. Things move or change all the time, because they are acted on by external forces. B moves C, and C moves D. The cause of D's movement was C, and the cause of C's movement was B. But how did B have the ability to move C? Well, maybe B was moved by A. But what caused A to move B? At some point, you just get to a cause that doesn't have an antecedent cause. If not, you just keep going back into infinity, and you never get to the start of the chain. The argument is that you can't go backwards forever. That's called an infinite regression. If you go backwards forever, you never get to the place where the chain started, and that's impossible.

JAY. I had read about this argument before, but only briefly. It was called The First Cause Argument when I read about it, and the author made it seem pretty simple, not to mention obviously wrong-headed. I remember that the argument was presented in the following way:

The author said that some Christians believe that every single thing needs a cause to account for its existence, and they track back through all things to arrive at God, who is supposed to be the first cause of everything. That sounds great, but if the logic of the first cause argument is that everything needs a cause, then that would mean that God would need a cause too. If God doesn't need a cause, then not every single thing needs a cause, and the logic of the first cause argument is shown to be faulty.

When I first heard that, I thought people must be pretty stupid to use the first cause argument, since it was so clearly self-contradictory. I couldn't believe that it was supposed to be one of the best and oldest arguments for the existence of God. Studying it more the last little while, I can't believe how much of a caricature that description is. Presenting the cosmological argument that way is to present a straw man. Beating the stuffing out of a straw man isn't that difficult, but it's also a waste of time!

RON. Yeah, I came across that type of caricature too. I've also come across versions of this argument that are really sophisticated, and really well defended. After reading some of the objections to these different versions, I've reached the conclusion that this argument needs to be taken really seriously. That "First Cause" parody is too common, and really unfortunate.

JAY. Okay, so that's a point of agreement right from the start. This ultimate questions of life stuff isn't that bad after all! Let's run over some of the forms of the argument, and some of the objections, just to cross reference our findings and ideas. Remember, we can honestly disagree, and we're doing our best to understand some really complicated philosophical arguments. We'll give the best reasons that we can to support our positions, but in the end we both know there's much that we don't know, and we're not exactly experts; or at least not yet, anyway.

RON. Sounds good. Do you want to start with the older versions of the argument, or do you want to start with some of the more modern ones and see if we have time for the older versions later?

JAY. Well, you've already mentioned how the argument from motion was presented by the Greeks. How about we start with the argument that I kept coming across in recent journal articles? It's called the *kalam* cosmological argument.

RON. Great, I wrote down the premises of that argument. William Lane Craig has presented the argument in the following form: 1. Everything that begins to exist has a cause; 2. The Universe began to exist; 3. Therefore the universe has a cause. He notes that this is a deductive syllogism, so that if his first two points are in fact true, the conclusion absolutely has to be true as well. So the only question is whether or not the first two statements are true. If they are, then the universe is an effect which must have a cause.

JAY. Premise number one states that everything that begins to exist has a cause. Honestly, it seems impossible to argue with that. I don't think anyone could honestly live in the world with the governing idea that things can come into existence without causes. If things just come into existence without any reason or cause, well, that just doesn't make any sense. Why would anyone deny that premise? The only other alternative is to argue that things can come from nothing.

RON. Doesn't it seem obvious that things *can't* come from nothing? Nothing. No *thing*. Nothing is not a principle, a force, a particle, or a speck of matter. It isn't anything. *Some*-thing does not come from *no*-thing! How could a particle, energy, or any other thing that is a thing come from nothing? It's simply not possible. To argue otherwise is to misunderstand what the word nothing means—at least as far as I can tell. Arguing theoretically that something can come from nothing, and then arguing practically that something actually did come from nothing seems pretty far-fetched. That's definitely a position for which there's no proof.

JAY. Denying that first premise seems pretty weird. Even if something could come from nothing, there certainly is no proof that it did, as you said. But some people have seriously said that this is just a chance, random universe, and so strange things can happen all the time. I have to admit, though, that something coming from nothing wouldn't just seem strange, it would seem impossible. The real question comes down in the second premise: Did the universe come into existence, or is it eternal?

If the universe is eternal, then it did not come to exist, and therefore falls outside the syllogism of the *kalam* argument. I'm not the world's leading authority in science, but I do know that the majority opinion of scientific scholars is that the universe came into existence about thirteen billion years ago, give or take a few weeks! Even professional scientists admit that the origins of the universe are shrouded in mystery, and that we just frankly don't know precisely how or what things were like at the beginning. But scientists say that somehow there was something, and in a Big Bang it blew up and has been expanding as our universe ever since. At least that's what most scientists teach us, and that's what most people accept today. That strange event is seen as the beginning of the space/time universe, which was something that didn't exist before.

RON: For those people who believe that the universe may simply be eternal despite Big Bang cosmology, William Lane Craig presents a mathematical treatment which shows why the universe can't be of eternal age. His argument against an infinite regress of time seems clear and intuitively obvious. This idea of an infinite regress being impossible is vital to the cosmological argument.

JAY. Yeah, I came across the impossibility of an infinite regress all the time in my readings about this argument. If every effect needs a cause, you keep going back further and further until you come to something that doesn't need a cause. If you don't arrive at something that doesn't need a cause, you just keep going back further and further on into infinity, and that's impossible.

RON. Craig argues that if you go back in time one second, two seconds, three seconds, all the way back through an infinite past, you'd never get to the end of the line, because you could always add one more second. Three billion seconds yields to three billion and one, and on and on you'd go forever. But if you went on forever, you'd never get to the end of the line, and if you never got to the end of the line, how would you start moving towards the present? It's impossible to start at one and count to infinity, and it's just as impossible to start at negative one and count to infinity the other way. If we called the present "0 seconds" and we said there was an infinite number of seconds in the past that had to be counted down until we could get to the present 0, that would be just as absurd as someone telling you they just finished counting from one to the end of infinity. So there can't be an infinite amount of past seconds. Time had to have a beginning, and that would coincide with the beginning of the universe.

JAY. An objection to that idea, however, comes from people who say that actual infinite sets of time really do exist. As an example, between one second and two seconds there lies an infinite amount of decimal points, so that an infinite number of second fragments are passed between one second and two seconds. This means that it is possible to have a real infinite set of time, and still get to the present.

RON. Oh, that sounds kind of like the riddle about the rabbit catching up to the turtle, or the airplane never getting to its destination, because it has to cross half the distance from point A to point B, and then half the distance again, and then half the distance again, and since you're always only crossing half the distance, you logically never arrive. That drives people crazy, because it seems that logic dictates that you can never arrive, or that the rabbit never catches up, but clearly in real life you can get to your destination. What you need in those cases is to apply the category of time. If you can move sixty miles an hour, then once an hour has elapsed you have traversed sixty miles. There is a relationship between time and distance traveled that relates to both of those riddles.

That gets a little trickier in the case of time alone, like in the *kalam* argument. Yet it seems just as much like a riddle as the other illustrations. It's one thing to say the rabbit never catches up, and it's another thing to actually *believe* the rabbit never catches up. Even if the theory is tricky, the reality is as obvious as could possibly be.

Really though, I think it's apples and oranges. The argument against an infinite regress is dealing with whole numbers, or at least the same unit of measurement. That there exists an infinite number of decimal places between one and two seems obviously true, but just as obviously there does not exist an infinite amount of the same decimal number between one and two. There is not an infinite amount of quarters (0.25) between one and zero, nor is there an infinite number of tenths. There isn't an infinite number of any one decimal point, no matter how large or small. If you pick one stable unit of measurement, there can only exist a finite amount of it.

For this argument, that would mean that as long as the unit of measurement is stable and uniform, you can only have a finite amount of it. The contention is that the past does not consist of an infinite number of whole seconds. Whatever you do with decimal places seems irrelevant to that fact. Someone needs to show how there can be an infinite number of seconds in the past in order for this argument to fail. In fact, I think a major difference is drawn between the existence of an infinite set and the creation of an infinite set through successive addition. Craig points this out. Abstractly, an infinite amount of decimal places exists between the numbers one and two. But you can never make an infinite set by always adding one more member to it. In the case of time, this means that you can never reach an actual infinite by continuing to add one to one to one forever. Theoretically, then, the math of the *kalam* argument proves that the universe has not existed for an infinite amount of time, and this is added to the pronouncements of the scientists who say that the space/time universe came into existence in the past.

JAY. It's amazing that people use math and science to think about the existence of God. How many times have you heard that faith is totally opposed to science, thinking, and facts? On the same topic of science and math, I've also heard people apply the second law of thermodynamics to the age of the universe. When you read science texts you discover that the majority scientific opinion is that the universe is using up its supply of heat energy, and when all the energy is evenly distributed across the universe, the whole universe will become a lifeless place. It's the law of entropy. It also means that there is a finite amount of energy that can be used in the universe.

Nobody really denies that this is true; in fact, there is no reason to deny it. Entropy is a fact. The difficulty this creates for people who believe the universe is infinitely old is that there is only a finite amount of energy, and it is being used up. A finite amount of energy would have been swallowed up in the supposed infinite amount of time in the past. How could a finite amount of energy last for an infinite amount of time? Of course it can't last forever, which is why scientists predict that heat death is coming up. Nobody is foolish enough to argue that our universe's finite energy reserves will last for an infinite amount of time into the future. What would make someone think that a finite amount of energy would have lasted through an infinite eternity of time in the past?

RON. That's something I've never thought of. I don't know enough about the laws of thermodynamics to be authoritative on this one, but I certainly have heard scientists predict this future state of energy depletion, where all the energy in the universe has been used up, with the result that the universe dies. In fact, some atheists argue that there cannot be a God because he would have designed a better universe that wouldn't end up that way. Admitting that point, though, seems to mean that the universe did begin to exist, and whatever begins to exist has a cause. What would cause the universe?

JAY. Really, if God did make the universe, I don't see why he couldn't intervene to stop it from ultimately reaching that state of entropy. So I don't see how that objection about faulty design is compelling, but I do see how admitting that the universe will end up this way does drive you to the conclusion that the universe has only existed for a finite amount of time. Unless the universe came into existence for no reason and out of nothing, which is impossible once we understand what *nothing* actually means, it seems inescapable that there must have been a cause for the existence of the universe.

RON. This all seems neat and tidy, but almost too neat and tidy. There are some objections to this argument. Let's discuss some of them.

JAY. Okay, first there's the argument that the cosmological argument is based on something called "the Principle of Sufficient Reason." This principle means that if something happens, there is a sufficient reason for its happening. Some people have objected that the Principle of Sufficient Reason isn't necessarily true, and until it has been proven to be true, the whole argument is based on an uncertain axiom.

RON. Right. So in other words, the argument is that things can happen without any reason at all to account for them. What's the alternative: "the Principle of Insufficient Reason"?

JAY. I don't know, but that's an objection that people have seriously made. To me it's about as forceful as the idea that things can come from nothing, or that effects don't require causes. If things don't need a sufficient reason to happen, why bother with thinking or investigating? You could never know whether or not something was happening because of something else, or whether it was just happening without a sufficient reason to explain it. I'll stick to believing that when things happen, there is a reason for it.

RON. In my judgment, a more forceful objection comes from those who claim that if this principle of causality were to be universally true, you end up with a logical contradiction when it comes to God. I know it sounds like that first objection we mentioned at the very beginning, but does the cause of the universe need a cause too? Nothing that exists could cause itself—be a self-caused being—because to be a cause you have to exist. So a self-caused being would have to exist before it could cause itself to exist! God can't be self-caused.

JAY. Nobody that I read argues that God is *self*-caused. They argue that God is *un*-caused. Like the Unmoved Mover. There must be a being which simply isn't caused, not by others or even itself. It exists because somehow existence is inherent in its very nature. This is what sets up some of those complicated arguments about necessary and contingent beings, which we're both sure we don't want to get into. We've already seen that the universe isn't the ultimate cause, since it began to exist, so there must be at least one cause beyond it. As far as whether or not the cause of the universe needs a cause, I can't see how that's extremely relevant, because at some point you have to reach the end of that chain of causes. Eventually you have to come to a cause that is uncaused. All we know at this point is that if science tells us anything about the origins of the universe, it is that the universe came into existence, and so it can't be the first cause. Other ideas about the origins of the universe, like the Oscillating model, and the paradigms that postulate vacuums and energy fluxes, are simply not widely endorsed by the broader scientific community.

RON. Another objection that I came across is called the fallacy of composition. Apparently it's a logical fallacy to conclude that if the parts contain a certain characteristic, the whole has to contain it too. Examples include a hockey team with five great players, but the team itself isn't great. I've seen that many times, where a sports team gets a roster that looks unbeatable on paper, all the athletes are great individually, but as a team they're not great at all. Put another way, while it is true that every human being has a mother, that doesn't mean that the whole human race has a mother. What's true of the parts isn't necessarily true for the whole. Applied to the cosmological argument, the objection is that every individual thing needs a cause, but that doesn't mean that everything as a whole needs a cause.

JAY. I didn't come across that objection. How do people answer it?

RON. Well, someone pointed out that the fallacy of composition is an informal fallacy, and that means that while the whole might not have the attributes of the parts, it also might. That sports team with five great individual players may be lousy as a whole, or it might be great. If every tile is blue, putting down fifty tiles to make a floor gives you a blue floor. Each tile is the color blue, and the whole floor is that color too. Every individual part needs a cause, and the whole thing might need a cause, too.

Frankly, though, after what we've talked about so far, it seems to me that the universe has been shown to need a cause, so even the fallacy of composition just doesn't seem to apply to the *kalam* version of this argument. The universe came into existence, and it didn't come from nothing. I don't want to impugn anyone's motives, but it seems that maybe people object to where this argument points because they don't like the implications. If the universe needs a cause—well, maybe we're happier thinking that there's nothing beyond the space/time universe that we know.

JAY. When you think about it though, it does seem too easy. The existence of God is supposed to be really mysterious. Many people say you can't know if God is real, and many people say there is no good evidence for his existence at all. Then when you're presented with this type of an argument, it seems too slick. How could it be that easy? You don't want to get too hasty either, because saying the universe has a cause is not at all the same as saying that the cause is God, or then saying which God that happens to be.

RON. I agree with that. It does go a long way to opening up my mind, though, about the possibility that God is real. The cosmological argument is simple, and it makes sense out of our experience. All objections to it seem pretty far-fetched, at least to what I consider to be commonsense. Maybe if you decided that God couldn't be real you'd have to find something wrong with an argument that points in the direction of something existing that's bigger than our universe. The only problem is that seems to be where the evidence points.

JAY. It's been an interesting start, that's for sure. I've enjoyed discussing these things together, although I doubt that we'll be able to agree about everything as easily as we've agreed about things today. So the next time we get together we're discussing arguments from design?

RON. Yep, if that's still fine with you. I'm more excited about these studies than ever.

JAY. Just before we go, though, it's important to see exactly where we are. At this point I can say that, with what I understand, it seems that the universe needs a cause. What that cause is, I don't know. The cosmological argument doesn't tell me if one religion is true, or even what type of force the cause of the universe could be.

RON. Some people develop the argument much further, arguing that the cause of the universe clearly must be very powerful, smart, and personal, since personal beings exist in the universe. These implications are much more tentative, though. Yet I have to admit that it does seem like the cause of the universe would have to have some of the qualities or characteristics that we usually ascribe to God. Then again, maybe we just don't know enough about the conditions at the beginning of the universe to know what really happened. I will admit that the most logical thing to me seems to be that this argument indicates that the universe, with our current state of understanding, needed a cause to come into existence. Definitely more arguments would be required to make this cause identical with one of the versions of God found in the major world religions.

JAY. Well, let's leave those sorts of matters alone for right now. I think we both have enough to mull over for the time being. I'm sure we'll discover lots more fascinating stuff as we get ready for next time!

2

The Teleological Argument

JAY. Hey, Ron. Good to see you again. Our last conversation really made me think, but once I started reading some of the arguments about how the universe bears the marks of having been designed, I was more interested than ever.

RON. Exactly the same thing happened to me. When I left last time I went home and thought about what we had talked about. It was really beneficial to think about, to mull it over in my mind some more. Then I started researching the teleological argument, and I couldn't believe how much of it is based on statistics and scientific facts. Obviously the crucial issue is how one interprets those facts, but the data is the same for all sides. I found that really interesting.

JAY. I was really taken by surprise when it came to how wide ranging the data in this argument is. Philosophers look at statistics and scientific facts from the universe as a whole, from galaxies, from the position of our earth to the sun, from the earth's environment, ecosystems, and more. And as if that's not enough, they look at the intricacies of all the systems in the body, how all the body parts function together, and then they go to the microscopic level and deal with cellular systems as well. The teleological argument involves looking at the universe as a whole, and then goes all the way down to looking at DNA and RNA.

RON. It really is amazing how much this argument covers, but I guess it has to have a huge explanatory scope because the basic premise of the argument is that the universe, and everything in it, was designed to accomplish certain goals or ends. I found out that the word telos means goal or end, and teleological is based on that root word. So the argument is that the universe and everything in it was designed in a specific way so that certain things could be accomplished.

This is a basic principle for how the world as we know it operates. When we see a car driving down the road, we just take it for granted. When we see a car pulled over on the side of the highway with its hood up and smoke coming out of it, we know there's something wrong! The car isn't functioning the way the designer wants it to.

JAY. A couple of centuries ago a man named William Paley was one of the most vigorous proponents of this argument. Although the argument is much more advanced now, the basic premise is still largely the same. He said that if you saw a watch, with all of its intricate parts working together for the purpose of telling time, you'd know that it was designed and built especially for the purpose of time telling. It didn't just happen to randomly and accidentally come together in such an amazingly detailed way for such an exact purpose. Such an incredible relationship of working parts producing a specific end screamed out that it was built specifically for that very purpose, and that in turn meant that there must have been a designer.

Just like cars or trucks today. When you think about all the parts working together, like the internal combustion engine, the steering wheel, the ignition, the frame, the gas lines, the exhaust pipe, the gearshift, and all the rest, you recognize that this piece of machinery was designed and built on purpose. There's no way it could just accidentally assemble itself into such a working order.

RON. I just wish cars were better designed! Or maybe they could use fewer parts. I had to take my car into the shop last week, and I got a lesson in how much it costs to keep intricately connected parts in working order, so that I can accomplish my goal of driving across town!

JAY. Yeah, is it really possible that my $3,000 used car contains $10,000 worth of parts? How does that happen?

RON. I don't know, but I guess our vehicles are complex systems of systems. Each individual system has to function by itself, and then all the systems also have to function together. That's pretty complex interaction.

JAY. Alright, well here's a suggestion. Last time we talked the most about the fact that the universe came into existence, and so needed a cause. Since we were talking about the whole universe then, let's start our discussion about the argument for the design of the whole universe, and then narrow our discussion to the design of the earth, then human beings, and then things at the cellular level. That seems like a logical progression to me, but we can do whatever you'd like.

RON. Sounds like a good design. Get it?

JAY. Unbelievable.

RON. Sorry. Let's just move on.

JAY. Okay, I know that we both wrote down some statistics for this discussion. There were so many numbers they boggled my mind. I could never memorize them in a million years. Do you want to take turns sharing really mind-boggling facts?

RON. Sure. You go first.

JAY. All right, here we go. In the cosmological argument, we saw that the existence of the universe points to a creator. Since the Big Bang is the model that we were taught in school to explain the expansion of the universe, let's look at what this event was supposed to involve in order to determine whether or not its results appear to be more the product of chance or the work of an intelligent designer.

RON. Sure, let's go with that. I have to admit though, in studying some of these arguments from design, it seems that some scientists just won't accept even the possibility of the existence of God, even when the evidence points that way. Scientists seem to have an agenda like everyone else. I think sometimes that agenda might even interfere with the models they teach.

JAY. Even a cursory reading of the history and philosophy of science shows how many times data was misinterpreted because the 'objective' scientist couldn't see past their own preconception of the way things had to be. Paradigms can control how data is interpreted. If an experiment doesn't support the paradigm, a lot of times it's called an anomaly, and written off. Eventually the anomalies build up so high that they can't be ignored, and the paradigm itself is reworked. This has happened over and over and over again. When you look back you're amazed that they kept working on the scaffolding of an obviously flawed framework, but it often takes decades or even centuries for the scientific community to acknowledge where the facts really point. That is simply a fact of history.

Let's go on to the topic at hand, though. Working backwards from the state of the universe today, all the matter in the universe was reduced to a point of incredible density, which thirteen billion years ago exploded and resulted in the universe as we know it. At the moment of explosion, however, the matter had to have just the perfect amount of density, out of the trillions and trillions of possible densities it could have had. If the difference had been marginally higher, the universe would have collapsed long before life had formed. If the difference was even the slightest part smaller, the expansion of the universe would have been so rapid that stars and planets could never have formed.

So, on a secular model, this point of ultra dense matter appeared from nothing—without any reason behind it at all—and then exploded, expanded, and just happened to be so constituted that it had the only one out of billions and billions of possible make-ups that could allow it to expand so that the production of human life wasn't simply impossible right from the start. The precision required for this balance, out of all the possible combinations, is so amazingly tuned to the one setting that could produce life that the 'dial' seems to have been purposely set to this finely tuned balance in order for the telos of life to be achieved.

RON. In other words, there's no explanation for why the universe began to exist in the first place, and then there's no explanation for why the universe would be able to produce life. The odds are so far stacked against it that it's virtually impossible!

I was reading that the carbon molecule, which is the basis of all organic life, including human life of course, could not possibly have formed if the temperature of the Big Bang fireball had been a trillionth of a degree colder or hotter. Can you believe the luck involved in that for human life? Nobody I know would buy a lottery ticket if the odds were one in a trillion. And that's on top of your stat! I got out my calculator, and I assumed that the population of the earth was seven billion. If we multiplied the earth's population 143 times, we'd have just over one trillion people. So, someone tells you that you need to go into a world that has 143 times the earth's population, and pick one random person. If you pick that one person, it's not impossible that life can begin—which isn't of course the same thing as life actually beginning. But if you don't pick the right person, life won't begin for sure because it can't begin. What would you think if you randomly chose that one person? Taken with your statistic, just to get our universe, and the possibility of a carbon molecule, we're at odds of less than 1 in 1,000,000,000,000, not just once, but twice! That's a tall order for chance.

JAY. Check this out. If our sun were 5% closer, the earth would be a furnace like Venus. That's not much room for change. But if the sun were 1% farther away, the earth would be engulfed in a perpetual ice age. No life would have formed either way.

That's just the beginning. Absolute precision in fine-tuning is also seen in the gases that compose the earth's atmosphere, the temperature and amount of water, the size and intensity of the sun, and even the emergence of plant life at just the right time in the history of the universe to keep conditions right on earth for the production of animal life. We could literally go on and on and on, since the conditions have to be perfect each time, and the odds of perfection are millions, billions, and trillions to one. And they all have to be perfect!

RON. Let's slow down. Before we go any further, let's recap the underlying logic in the secular Big Bang model. Scientists look at this event that happened thirteen billion years ago, with all of the amazingly impossible odds against it ever happening in the first place, and then they add to it the impossibility of this accidental and purposeless event having the perfect coordinates to allow for the existence of human life, and they conclude that there was no designer? So, the idea is that a universe popped into existence out of nothing for no reason, and it just happened to be a universe which would have the one in a trillion trillion odds of being capable of producing human life?

So, not only was it possible for this universe to support human life, but once this universe actually existed, against all odds, dust and gases shot out for thirteen billion years on a trajectory that was so perfect that our earth formed with just the right conditions for human life to thrive. The chemical composition and speed of the expansion just happened to accidentally be perfect. Then, on this miracle planet, in this miracle universe, life emerged from non-living matter against all odds, and then became human. Again, life just happened to begin, with no purpose, no guidance, and no plan. The odds against life starting on earth, even after you get the earth into existence, are billions to one, if not much more. How lucky can we get?

JAY. I think I can sense some sarcasm there! What's fascinating is that once we make that move from the universe and the balance between our world and the sun with all the precision of the atmospheric properties, to the constitution of human beings, we are moving from the less complex to the more complex! Although human beings are an infinitesimally small entity compared to the universe, there is nothing more complex than a human being. A human genome is far more complex than the whole universe. The odds against one assembling randomly are astronomical. The numbers are so huge that even though I read them I can't even fathom what they are!

RON. Well, if they're bigger than the odds against the universe being able to produce human life, they must be huge. Quite honestly, after looking at these statistics—and this is only a small, representative part of the data—I just can't see how this world could be an accident. That we actually exist at all, or that the universe actually exists at all, is just mind-boggling. To think that the universe has supposed to have been expanding mindlessly for thirteen billion years, and out of the almost infinite number of possibilities for what the universe could have been like, we end up with the one where human life could possibly be produced, and then human life actually happened to get produced! I honestly don't know anyone in the whole world who would accept those odds for anything else. It seems that some people are just opposed to thinking that the universe wasn't an accident.

JAY. An illustration that I came across really helped me put these odds into perspective. Pretend that you walked into the control center for the universe. Let's say there are one hundred dials, and that each one controls a physical law in the universe. One controls the strength of gravity, another controls electromagnetic interactions, and so on. Now, the first control has five hundred possible settings. In order for human life to have the possibility of being produced, the first knob has to be set at 51. You look, and that's where it's set. The next control has to be set at either 1000 or 1001, out of

5000 possible settings. Again, that's where it happens to be. The next knob has to be set somewhere between 12657.4, and 12657.9. For this knob, there are one hundred thousand possibilities. Lo and behold, the knob is set exactly at 12657.6.

Now, you keep going through all the controls, and each has to have a precise setting in order for human life to even be possible. Yet, each of the one hundred controls is perfectly set, against all conceivable odds. The question is, would you think that these controls just accidentally happened to have these settings, or would you think they were purposefully set? Honestly, if this question didn't involve the existence of God, absolutely nobody would believe that such fine-tuning could possibly happen without an intelligent being purposefully setting the exact coordinates on the controls. In the final analysis, the odds of the controls all being set to a place where human life can exist is one out of 10,000,000,000 with the exponent 123. To put it in perspective, that last number is larger than the total number of elementary particles in the entire universe.

Up until a little while ago, I would have said that science had it all figured out. But the more I've read, the more I'm beginning to see that scientists have an agenda as well. Here's an example. Francis Crick is half of the Watson-Crick duo who had an incredible breakthrough in studying the DNA molecule. That's as good as it gets when it comes to a scientist's credentials! Not too long ago he reported that the condition of the world before life began made it impossible for life to form here on earth. In other words, the whole process that's absolutely necessary for the theory of evolution couldn't have gotten started! That's a huge claim. And since Crick's a scientific authority, what could you do but listen up? But then he went on to float out a theory called panspermia. Basically, he suggested that life must have evolved somewhere else, and then sophisticated aliens "air" mailed the seeds of life to earth.

Even though the only evidence he had for the origins of life here on earth precluded evolution, he couldn't get past that. He was already committed to having a universe where life only emerged due to evolutionary factors. When the evidence didn't support this, he just transferred evolution's origins to a planet no one has ever discovered. Why not just say that maybe if life didn't start on earth through accidental means, they should look for different theories? You can suggest aliens, but if you suggest God, or even a generic intelligent designer, you get mocked as being unscientific. That really surprised me.

RON. Actually, stuff like that used to surprise me, but now it doesn't really surprise me anymore. An argument has been made that evolution might fall prey to something known as irreducible complexity. This means that there are some systems in the world that are too complicated to take apart and still have them function. A famous example is of cilia in some single cell organisms. By the way, single cell organisms are not single parted! Some consist of hundreds of parts, all of which must function together.

The doctrine of Evolution is very particular. Everything that is complex had to get that way through small, tiny modifications. Nothing that is complex could just start that way. Since Evolution demands accidental, incremental changes which allow for the species to survive, each step along the way to the development of an organ like the heart, or a system like the cardiovascular system, had to all individually be helpful. An irreducibly complex system would be one where without two, three, or more parts, the whole system is worthless. But all the parts depend on each other for their effectiveness. So the question becomes, How did all of the necessary parts happen to appear and function together all at exactly the same time, when the Theory of Evolution only allows for small, slight modifications over time?

JAY. Wait a minute, what about Punctuated Equilibrium? That says that as the species evolved they didn't just go through small, gradual changes, they sometimes went through huge leaps in one generation. New Darwinists have been arguing that slight, successive, mutations can't account for where we are today. Some evidence points away from those gradual, almost imperceptible mutations that result in macroscopic evolutionary development.

RON. Right, that's what they say. Old-line Darwinists don't accept that theory. The truth is Punctuated Equilibrium is a theory designed to explain away why there are so many gaps in the fossil record. According to Darwin, the fossil record should be overflowing with the link species that would be required to fill in the gaps between all the species on earth. Remember, the whole theory is that every single species in the history of the planet came from one parent cell. So there needs to be huge amounts of fossils that represent life forms in-between one species and another known species. When the fossil record failed to show the thousands and thousands of fossils like these that the Theory of Evolution demanded be there, instead of admitting that Evolution was not being supported by the data, people just changed the Theory. Unfortunately for the evolutionists, Darwin's Theory needs small, gradual, slight modifications. Huge leaps, without any know explanation, is a pretty desperate move.

JAY. So basically Punctuated Equilibrium is a position to explain why there isn't any evidence, instead of a position that works with the evidence we have?

RON. I guess you could put it that way. The irony here is that New Darwinists are saying that the scientific evidence proves that evolution didn't happen slowly, as Darwin thought. Old Darwinists are saying the scientific evidence proves that evolution couldn't happen fast, as in Punctuated Equilibrium. Creationists are simply saying that they're both right. Macroscopic evolution didn't happen slowly, and it couldn't happen fast. God created this world order, and life forms.

JAY. When you don't believe that God exists, I suppose you have to think that natural explanations exist for everything in the universe. I've heard people say that since Evolution is true, and since God isn't real, it is illegitimate to appeal to God just because we can't really explain some things on the basis of science. They'd say that over time science would find the answers. Appealing to God was supposed to be laziness or ignorance. You know, faith not fact. But if the facts point towards intelligent design, isn't it ignorant to say that they don't? If science doesn't have the answers right now, isn't it a matter of faith to say that science will have the answers tomorrow? All the theories against irreducible complexity are pure speculation. They basically assume that systems aren't really irreducibly complex, and then they offer all sorts of possible scenarios for how something which seems irreducibly complex could have gotten that way. It becomes a game of "let's see which naturalistic explanation accounts for the most evidence," instead of an impartial inquiry into what actually happened. Lots of theories, and lots of speculation, but no proof. That's not how we're told science works. We're told that science is all about facts, all about what can be proven for sure. I guess it doesn't work that way. Scientists have their commitments and philosophical leanings just like everyone else. Panspermia, Punctuated Equilibrium, faith in science: it sounds more like doctrine and faith than experiment and objectivity!

RON. Honestly, I agree with you. You see this when some people try to argue that, despite the appearance of design, the universe doesn't have a designer. Some say that this can't be the only universe, that there must be trillions of other ones. If there are trillions and trillions of other ones, then of course one would have these conditions. The problem with this, of course, is that this is the only universe we know of! Instead of looking at the evidence in this universe and accepting that the evidence points to design, people see that but won't accept the conclusion, so they multiply trillions of universes that nobody has any evidence for at all. Then we go home and say how mature, reasonable, and scientific we are not to believe in God.

JAY. I have to admit, looking at the stats makes me think that the evidence points more towards a purposeful design than a random, accidental, meaningless universe that happens to exist against all odds and happened to produce human life against even greater odds! Maybe it's a commitment to naturalism and an unwillingness to consider the existence of God that leads some people to their conclusions. I mean, if you're only allowed or willing to consider "natural" causes, then all the data needs to be interpreted in naturalistic ways. But it doesn't seem like the data obviously supports antisupernaturalism. Perhaps there is no designer: but you can't say that it's irrational to think that there might be, or even that there is one.

RON. Here's something else to consider, just for fun. If Evolution is true, how do we even know that our brains work? I mean, Evolution is about survival of the fittest. Maybe the world is so psychologically harsh, that those who survive the longest are the ones who can't really understand what it's really like. Maybe all of our brains evolved for survival, and they can't really comprehend truth. Darwin even struggled with this. He said he was tormented by the thought that since he wouldn't trust a monkey's brain to know the truth, he had no good reason to trust his own brain, since it came from a monkey. As far as the Theory of Evolution is concerned, if naturalistic evolution is true, you could never know that the world isn't just a huge insane asylum. Everyone in an insane asylum thinks that they're intelligent, and they think that everyone else is crazy. I'd like to hear an evolutionist explain to me how they know that their brain can be trusted! To do so, of course, they'd have to use their brain, and that becomes a vicious circle.

JAY. Well, now that you mention it, how did thinking arise from non-thinking matter? I mean, we are reflective, self-conscious, sentient beings. But if the whole universe is just matter, accidentally milling around and accidentally coming together, how could sentience emerge from a matrix where nothing is sentient? How does intelligence emerge from non-intelligence? How does thinking emerge from blocks of matter that are incapable of thought? If someone told me that in one billion years the rocks would be thinking, or that willow trees would be getting Ph.D.'s I'd have to laugh. Intelligence doesn't come from non-intelligent matter!

RON. You know, I never thought of it quite like that before. And how does my evolutionist friend know that their brain works? That's actually pretty tough.

JAY. I have a suggestion for you. Next week an atheist is giving a presentation at the university about why God can't exist. Do you want to go? After that, maybe we could talk about what he had to say.

RON. Sure. I mean, we're looking for truth, so let's hear all sides. Remember, the pursuit of truth requires an open mind. After today's discussion, however, it seems that many people aren't open-minded enough to even consider the existence of God, no matter how neatly the evidence would fit with his existence. If God is real, and if he created the universe and designed it for human habitation, all of those incredibly astronomical statistics make perfect sense—it's what we'd expect to find. Only someone really close-minded wouldn't acknowledge that, even if they wanted to investigate the arguments more closely.

JAY. I know that there's lots more that could be discussed about this, like the idea of specified complexity. We recognize an intelligent design when we see information that is both specified or logically ordered, and complex. A jumble of twenty-six random letters is complex, but unspecified. A pattern of b's and c's like bbccbbbcbcbccccbb is specified, but not complex. The alphabet, set out from a to z is both specified and complex. When you see that, you know that it didn't get ordered that way by random accident. DNA is like this. It is both highly specified and highly complex, and so according to information theory it shows the marks of intelligent design.

RON. Now, there are some objections to this argument which we haven't touched on, but I know we have to get going. Let me just throw out one quick one, if that's okay.

JAY. Sure, go ahead.

RON. Some people have argued that if the universe requires a designer because it functions in such a complex way, then God must need a designer too, because he functions even better. Basically, the objection is that the principle that function requires design necessitates God needing a designer too. I think there are several ways this has been answered. But without getting into that, just like in the cosmological argument, it seems safe to say that the existence of this universe requires a cause, and the complexity of the universe and things in it are best explained by purposeful design. The existence and complexity of God would be of a qualitatively different kind. I wish we had more time to talk that through, but that's enough for right now.

JAY. Great. So we're on for that presentation? Let's meet in the lobby fifteen minutes before the presentation, and then we'll get good seats.

RON. Sounds good. See you there.

3

Why God Does Not Exist

MR. ALLEN. Hello everyone. My name is Mr. Allen, and I'm here tonight to tell you why I am convinced that God does not exist. That sounds like a harsh claim. That may even sound like an arrogant claim. How do I, a finite, fallible, small human being *know* for sure that God does not exist? How could anyone, in our postmodern times, presume to stand outside of their own subjective, finite experience, and seriously put forth the grand claim that there is no God in the universe? Well, tonight I'm going to tell you.

I could talk about different things tonight. I could talk about the Theory of Evolution, which is not a theory but a fact. Evolution has demonstrated that life emerged without the creative work or supervision of God. We know how the universe started, we know how life began, and we know how we got here today. Science has answered all our big questions, and God was not one of the answers. This alone leads me to confidently assert that God does not exist. If he did, the evidence would point to him, and we would accept that conclusion. Believe me, atheists and scientists are very open minded people, who, unlike people of faith, will only go with facts and reason. Where the data points, that's where we go!

For a number of reasons, however, I've decided not to talk about science tonight. I'm going to expose a problem for theism that can't be ignored. I'm going to demonstrate from history and from every day experience that a being like God simply cannot exist. God is supposed to be all-loving. He is supposed to be all-powerful. He is even supposed to be all-knowing, not just about things in the present, but also about things in the future. It must be nice to be that smart, strong, and good!

Yet when I look around at this world, and when I read books about history, I'm struck by one simple fact. This fact is as simple and obvious as it is clear and shocking. We're so used to it that it often gets ignored. Well, tonight I'm not going to let us ignore it. I'm going to hammer it into your heads. I'm going to hammer it into your hearts. I'm going to multiply example after example until you can't ignore it anymore. And once you're at that point, I'm going to ask you to consider whether or not a good, loving, kind, compassionate, wonderful God, who is also all-powerful and all-knowing, would allow this type of world to exist: A world which is full of pain, suffering, and death.

First, let's think about nature. Animals suffer horrendous pain every day. Predators cull out the weak, sick, old and young. Do you know how predators kill? Of course you do, but have you ever thought about it? Fangs and claws rip into flesh. Flesh is torn, punctured, mangled, and ruined. Many predators repeatedly wound their prey until they can go in for the final kill. Torn muscles, severed arteries, choking suffocation: these are the tools of the trade for the carnivore predators that exist all over our world, on the land, in the air, and swimming in the waters. As has been often said, nature is red in tooth and claw. Life flourishes through death, and death is painful and harsh.

At least for predators, the damage and pain they inflict accomplishes some good in that it keeps them alive. This, of course, simply ignores the fact that oftentimes predators only wound their prey, and the prey escapes to suffer and die without any benefit to the predator at all. But I digress.

What about pain in the animal kingdom that is of no value, not to even to predators?

For example, say that lightning strikes some dry timber and ignites a forest fire. As the blaze consumes more and more acres of the forest, more and more animals attempt to flee for their lives. The smoke gets thicker, the animals grow tired, and the blaze catches up with them. Animals of all sizes, large and small, mighty and weak, are overtaken by the flames and burned alive in the fire. Their deaths do not provide food for each other. Their deaths do not provide life for each other. Their deaths are not painless. They suffer intensely. They suffer in great panic and pain. There is no good reason for this to be, but it is. All-good? All-powerful? All-knowing? Would a wonderful being with the abilities of God allow such suffering; suffering which he could easily prevent?

It is not only animals that sometimes die in pointless, painful ways. I was reading just this morning about a poor young woman and her two year old baby son. She became pregnant as a teenager, and the father promised to love her and care for their child. Well, in what is an increasingly familiar story, the child was born, and the father took off, never to be heard from again. This poor young lady courageously did her best to care for her son, and she worked long hours in two different jobs to do it. After work one Friday night she put her son in the car and started driving towards her mother's apartment. In what could only be every parent's nightmare, she was so exhausted from working all week that she fell asleep behind the wheel. The car careened off the road, down an embankment, and into a stream swollen from the spring thaw. One brave passing motorist stopped his car and ran down to help. He managed to get the woman out of the car to safety, but he couldn't get the child out of the toddler restraints. He couldn't save him. Everyone who hears about this says that it was a terrible tragedy, and of course they're right. Everyone who hears about it wishes there was something they could do. Everyone knows that if they could have prevented this tragedy, they would have. Wouldn't *you* have prevented this tragedy if it was in your power to do so? If you could have saved this baby's life without risking any harm to yourself, and you just chose not to, wouldn't that mean that you were not a perfectly good person? In fact, isn't it true that only a morally contemptible being wouldn't have saved that baby's life if it were possible?

You will all undoubtedly recall the great tsunami on Boxing Day of 2004. Hundreds of thousands died. Hundreds of thousands more were seriously injured. Hundreds of thousands who survived lost absolutely all of their possessions, including their homes. Thousands of people were separated from their loved ones and from their friends and families. Many will never know if their loved ones are dead or alive. What a tragedy. What an absolutely horrendous state of affairs.

Think about the hurricane that devastated New Orleans. A whole city in the most powerful nation on the face of the earth destroyed overnight! The whole city is ruined. The whole population of half a million people is exiled. Families are separated. People die. People are injured. What a shame. I am willing to bet that many people listening to me tonight sent money for relief efforts after the tsunami and after Hurricane Katrina. Why did we send money for relief? Well, even though we couldn't *prevent* the tragedies from occurring we wanted to do our best to help people after they occurred. Really, what we were saying in donating to the relief efforts was that we wish it had never happened in the first place.

In Africa, and in many other nations, starvation routinely follows from crop failure due to lack of rain. Rain. Water falling from the sky is all that is required to keep millions and millions alive. Would you send that needed moisture if it was in your power to do so? Drops of water. Certainly that's not a tall order for someone who's all-powerful. Certainly that's something an all-loving and truly wonderful being would do. Why let them die? Why let them starve? Why let innocent children starve and end their days in disease and pain? For God all of this could be totally prevented, without any real effort or exertion. Yet turn on the evening news, watch charity commercials, and you'll see that this continues day after day after day.

Speaking of Africa, have you heard about the AIDS pandemic? Have you heard about the tens of thousands of poor children who have been orphaned because of this disease? Have you heard about the poverty and the ignorance? In South Africa witch doctors tell people with AIDS that if they rape a virgin they'll be cured of the disease. This causes the disease to spread more and more. People suffer, people die, and the children bear the brunt of their parents' mistakes. What about the child who contracts AIDS in the womb of her infected mother? Certainly this is a tragedy none of us would allow to continue. If only we were all-powerful! If only we were all-knowing! We would certainly be good enough, even though we're not perfect, to prevent this sort of thing from perpetuating itself.

I have to admit that natural disasters by themselves don't really make it impossible for a good God to exist. Natural disasters aren't the worst kinds of evil that we see. What about man's inhumanity to man? What about the history of the behavior of our race? Certainly if we were created in the image of God, and watched closely by him, things would be different.

What do we have in human history? Wars, fighting and pain. The younger generation hasn't really experienced the ravages of war like other generations have. We haven't seen the globe tilting in blood, destruction, and violence.

We haven't seen dozens of our friends go to war, and only a few returning. Homes destroyed. Crops ruined on purpose. People tortured to extract confessions and information. Lies and propaganda everywhere you turn. Might makes right. Nations willing to kill others, and to sacrifice their own so that a few privileged elite can enjoy even more power, or satiate even more of their lusts.

Hitler's Germany has got to be taken as conclusive proof that God doesn't exist. People were tortured because of their race. People were subjected to experimental medical tests to see what the human body could endure. Jews by the millions were cruelly captured, families were separated, and then they were worked to death or simply killed on the spot. Jewish mothers had to pick between children, knowing that the one they chose would die today and the other would die in the morning. I will not—no, I cannot—dwell on this too much. You are familiar, of course, with the grisly details of that dark period in human history. Who stopped the Nazi regime? It wasn't God, because he let them gain power in the first place. The Nazis were stopped because literally millions of brave, imperfect humans were willing to die to stop their atrocious reign. Even we were good enough to oppose Hitler with our limited amount of power and knowledge.

Where was God? I ask you again, slowly and with a heavy heart: Where was God?

Slavery is another reason why God can't be real. Slavery is one of the greatest blights in the history of mankind. Many white people, not least some of the most religious people in the Western world rounded up and exported the supposedly inferior blacks of Africa to build up the New World for the benefit of the white Christians. Skin pigmentation became the criterion for human value! If you're dark you aren't fully human, you're chattel. Your body can be used by the master for sex. Your body can be beaten if your body doesn't work 18 hours a day on a starvation diet. Your body can be separated by an ocean width from the bodies of your family members. Your body can be forcibly removed from your home, your village, your land, your nation. Your body can die in transit because of cramped conditions, no water, and too many contagious diseases that were contracted by sitting in everyone's feces and urine. Then your body can be dumped into the ocean offshore when you're dragged up for inspection and they find you're too sick to sell, or you're already a corpse.

How many of us read about the slave trade and feel sick to our stomachs? How many of use marvel at man's inhumanity to man? How many of us wish that we could go back and make everything okay? How many of us wish we could have prevented that from ever happening? How many of us wish we were all-powerful? If we were, slavery never would have happened.

I'm purposefully not going to be very graphic here, but think about all the spousal and child abuse that takes place across our nation every day. Children are sickly abused in sexual ways. Children are beaten so viciously that some are left disfigured for life, and crippled psychologically. Children are punished using methods that can only be described as cruel and unusual torture. Little children, trying to please mommy and daddy, told over and over and over again that they're little idiots, little failures, little good-for-nothings, little mistakes. Parents telling children that they wish they had never been born. Parents beating children and telling them that it's all their fault—daddy wouldn't beat you if you weren't such a bad little girl! Mommy wouldn't have to whip you with the belt and lock you in the cellar if you were a good boy! What excuse could God possibly have for watching every minute of the day, for seeing everything done behind locked doors, and for doing absolutely *nothing*?

Children are growing up abused, neglected, and hated. Look at what they turn to. Look at the proliferation of gangs and violence. Look at the brutality on our streets. Escapism in gangs, violence, drugs, and alcohol is rampant. It's the only alternative. Life is too hard on many of our young people to allow them to cope. They've been beaten up and thrown on the garbage heap. No wonder they seethe with a pent up rage that expresses itself in violence and other self-destructive manifestations. If I was all-good, all-powerful, and all-knowing, I would have made a world where these things couldn't happen. This means that an all-good, all-powerful, all-knowing being and this world are mutually exclusive.

Now, some of you may have read some philosophy of religion before. You know that not even informed atheists like myself believe anymore that the existence of an omniscient, omnipotent, completely perfect being and the existence of evil are logically contradictory in a formal sense. So I can't just stand up here and say that the existence of God and the existence of evil are explicitly illogical. They're not. Today, all the best atheists admit that there is no deductive logical contradiction arising out of that data. That's important, philosophically. To clarify, let me quote one of the finest atheistic philosophers of religion, William Rowe, who has written: "Some philosophers have contended that the existence of evil is *logically inconsistent* with the existence of the theistic God. No one, I think, has succeeded in establishing such an extravagant claim. Indeed, granted incompatibilism, there is a fairly compelling argument for the view that the existence of evil is logically consistent with the existence of the theistic God. (For a lucid statement of this argument see Alvin Plantinga)." In this important paragraph, Rowe admits that the theistic philosopher Alvin Plantinga has demonstrated—using the Free Will Defense, let me add—that the existence of evil and the existence of

God are just not logically contradictory. No atheistic philosopher, as Rowe points out, has succeeded in demonstrating how there is logical contradiction between the existence of God and the existence of evil.

Having said that, however, it does seem very difficult to figure out why there is so much pointless evil in this world. Is the evil in the world what we would expect to find if the universe was in fact created by a good, all-powerful, all-knowing being? I'd have to say no. So do many other people. Even if it's not formally illogical, it is hard to understand how God and all this evil could coexist. I'd say it's virtually impossible to understand. It just doesn't make sense to me. A good God makes a world full of evil. Why? For what purpose? How? No, such a God is surely incompatible with a world full of evil. As has often been said, if God exists, he must be the devil!

Now, I don't want you to get upset with me. I don't want you to think that I'm a bully, or a bad guy. I'm just pointing out some of the rather obvious facts of life that we tend to ignore. God could stop all this evil, pain, and suffering from occurring. Obviously he doesn't. It would seem that we only have a certain number of conclusions that we can draw from this reality.

First, we could say that God isn't really all-good. That would explain why there is some evil in the world, and why innocent creatures can experience pain. Second, we could say that God isn't really all-powerful. It seems that this is the track that many believers have taken. God loves everyone, and he'd really like to help, but he just can't do what's required. Third, we could say that God doesn't know everything. Some theologians, called open theists, argue that God doesn't know the future, because the future isn't logically knowable. This has the unfortunate side effect of turning God into a seeming bungler who accidentally makes huge mistakes as he goes blindly forward. In this model God isn't bad, he's just largely incompetent. In the fourth place, we could conclude that this God does exist, and that there is a good reason for evil to exist too. This is a logical possibility. I mean, it is possible that God has a good reason for allowing evil to exist. But let me say that I personally reject this position, largely because there just seems to be too much evil, and too much suffering. The most obvious answer, of course, is that God simply doesn't exist. This accounts for all the data of pain, suffering and evil. Suffering makes sense apart from God, and evolution helps us to see why suffering is part of the world as we find it.

In conclusion, let me repeat that if I were the sort of being that God is supposed to be, I wouldn't let this world decay into such a sickly state of evil and suffering. I don't suspect that many of you would, either. So when I think about what I would do if I had God's abilities and moral perfection, and I see that God does things very differently from me, I am driven to conclude that God isn't real. No matter what you think about me, I'm honestly a nice enough guy that I would prevent every person in the world from ever suffering, if only I had the ability to do so. So would you. I submit to you that so would God, if only he were real.

Thank you very much for listening to me. I know that it hasn't been a very positive message. I know that the information I've mentioned is fairly heavy, and it's easy to go away depressed. But don't go out that way! I honestly believe that things will get much better for the human race when we realize that God is not real, and that we have to figure things out for ourselves. If we can continue to develop our moral sensibilities, and react against suffering, evil, and pain, then eventually we will have made great strides towards eliminating those terrible things from our world. We need to have more faith in human kind! We can get better, and we will. The future can be brighter than the past and even than the present if we just work together. Humans can get along. We can treat each other with dignity and respect. Let's all go out and make the world a better place! We're not all-good, all-knowing, or all-powerful, but we can use our finite goodness, knowledge, and power, to make finite changes in this world for the better. Large changes can result from the accumulation of small changes, as evolution has so ably proven.

Thank you very much for your attention and patience. Please have a good night, and a safe trip home.

4

Evil, the World, and God

JAY. Hi Ron. What did you think about Mr. Allen's presentation? It wasn't quite what I thought it was going to be like, but he really did hammer home how much suffering there is in the world today.

RON. Well, I left that presentation feeling pretty down, like I told you that night. The world is full of suffering. It doesn't seem right. Mr. Allen's challenge at the end seemed to ring really hollow. More faith in man? Now we're back to faith! From what he was saying, I can't see one good reason why we should put our faith in man. After all, human beings provided his most despicable examples of evil. Why have faith in an obviously evil creature?

JAY. Yeah, that part didn't really resonate with me either. He just finished telling us how terrible our race was, and then he told us to expect better things for tomorrow. Much of history shows man getting more and more brutal, not better! Hitler's Germany was not very long ago. People are still alive today who lived through it. Germany was the most technologically advanced country in the world at that time. We think that the more education we get, or the more computers we build, the better we get as people. That's simply not true. Technology just allows us to be more destructive in our evil, and to spread it around more widely. A pervert could have child pornography in some photographs twenty years ago, and now anyone in the world with a computer can access it. The sickness of society has not been cured by our education and technological advances.

RON. I do have to admit, however, that while he certainly didn't have any answers or solutions, his presentation really did make me do some soul searching, and heavy studying. The argument from evil is so emotional it grips you, and it really seems to be the atheist's best argument by far.

JAY. Interestingly enough, it has been for centuries. This isn't a new argument, it's been around forever. Theists know about it, and have interacted with it, and still believe in God. Some people seem to think that people with faith in God have never thought about the existence of pain and suffering before. I found out that not only have they thought about it, they've written a lot about it too.

RON. Well, let's dive right in. Even if we don't fully agree with every argument, let's list some of them off. Do you want to go first?

JAY. Sure. One point made by believing philosophers was that our perspective is too small to allow us to see the whole instead of just the parts. An analogy exists with paintings. When I was young my parents took me to an art gallery. The guide always showed us the best spot to stand so that we could see the whole painting. Too far away and you couldn't see the details. Too close, and you just saw smudges of color and swirls.

The argument is that right now we're too close to the painting to make it out. All we see is a dark smudge, or a swirl of navy blue, and when we focus on that part the whole thing looks ugly. For the artist, however, who stands at just the right distance to gain the full perspective, the painting needs every single dash of color that it has. The dark tones bring out the bright hues. So the whole painting is more beautiful with the dark colors than it would be without them. By analogy, the whole creation is more beautiful with some of the dark colors of suffering in it than it would have been without them. We just lack the perspective to comprehend the whole thing, since we're finite.

RON. I can't see anyway that that argument could be defeated, even if it's not true. It doesn't prove anything for sure, but any time you objected to it, you'd just be reaffirming that your perspective is too limited to allow for total comprehension, since if you could totally comprehend everything, you wouldn't have that objection in the first place. That at least provides a possible answer to the problem of suffering. I'm not sure I'm totally comfortable with it, though, and I'm not sure why. Maybe if my perspective wasn't so limited I'd be able to see that it is in fact true, but right now I'm not so sure. I mean, if God was the artist, you'd think that he could probably make an extremely beautiful painting without all the colors of suffering.

JAY. Yeah, that seems to make sense. Even if it's not fully satisfying, it does give an indication that perhaps we're just not in the best position to appoint ourselves as the ultimate judges of the way things should be. And, on the other hand, it is also an analogy. Analogies are never exactly identical to the reality that they're being compared to, or they wouldn't be analogous in the first place. I think that if you press the details of that analogy it inevitably breaks down, but the main point is that our perspective and understanding is too limited to appreciate how everything looks in the eyesight of omniscience.

RON. Okay, here's another point, although it's somewhat similar. Evil actually makes the world a better place. I know that sounds crazy at first. Think about the hurricane and the disaster in New Orleans. Yes, that was a tragedy, but look at the heroism and generosity of the people who poured out their time, energy, money, and effort to help the people affected. People made huge sacrifices to help those who lost everything in the hurricane. Good was poured out to meet the need. When you think about it, the most awesome examples of goodness usually come against the most terrible examples of evil.

My grandfather fought in the Second World War, fighting to stop the atrocities of the Nazis. People willingly gave up their lives and died to defend the helpless and those who had been overpowered. Brave young men and women left home to do their part in the war effort against evil. Soldiers threw themselves on top of grenades to save the lives of their comrades. Soldiers won medals for bravery when they put their lives at risk to save an injured or endangered fellow fighter. We are proud of those people, because their acts of goodness shine all the brighter against the black backdrop of evil.

JAY. I know that we often draw inspiration from people who have beat all odds, and triumphed over adversity. There is no doubt that looking at how people respond to tragedy makes most of us want to be better people ourselves. We can draw courage and strength from their examples. But having said that, I'm not sure if that really answers why there is evil in the first place. I mean, it seems like there is some limited good that does come from evil, but everyone I know would gladly trade a heroic example for no suffering any day. And frankly I also think that for every example of heroism or courage in the face of suffering that we can point to, there is probably another example where suffering led to despair, pain, and defeat. Perhaps the world does need to contain as much evil and suffering as it does in order for us to grow as a race of beings, but somehow that doesn't seem quite right to me.

RON. Let me add just one thing, which I think shows that sometimes we think something is a terrible tragedy but it turns out to be a blessing in disguise. I know families where some of the children have mental and physical disabilities. When the parents found out that the children had these disabilities, they were quite upset. Later on, however, I've heard them say that their special child has taught them more about joy, love, and living life than they ever learned from anybody else. Many things are so bad that they seem pointlessly irredeemable, but in the end they really are great blessings. And the child with special needs that I'm thinking about really loves life!

JAY. All of this seems to hinge on us just not knowing what's best, and not recognizing how some evil can result in a greater good. It also seems like there's some pretty major differences in how this topic can be approached. If we are going to strictly use logic, there are all kinds of reasons why God could have allowed evil to exist in this world. If we weigh the case based on our emotions it becomes much more difficult to sort out. Somehow it just feels like there shouldn't be so much evil in the world.

RON. That's very interesting. My reactions to this topic have been more visceral than intellectual for sure. It really does seem to be as much about feeling as thinking, or maybe even more. We just *feel* like there's too much evil in the world. Proving that this is genuinely the case, however, is much more difficult. One of the main responses of theists to the problem of evil is to say that there is no evil, or pain, or suffering in the world that God doesn't have a good reason for allowing. We don't know the reason in every particular instance, but God does. Sometimes we do see how something that causes pain turns out to be a blessing, but in the times that we don't we can trust that God does. In this position, there is nothing illogical at all with God being all-good, all-powerful, and all-knowing, and real evil existing in the world.

JAY. One thing that I learned while studying this topic was that we need to think about systems of ethics if we are to try to understand the relationship between good and evil. There are all kinds of ethical systems, and all kinds of positions in moral philosophy. Some say that something is good if it leads to good consequences. So an event is bad if it leads to bad consequences, but it is good if it leads to good consequences. That's oversimplified, but it's basically accurate. Another main view is that something is good or bad regardless of the consequences. In this model, it is the inherent value of something that is the issue, not the consequences that it produces.

A famous example of this difference is found in the question of whether or not lying is ever justified. Some say that it is, because a lie can produce good consequences and stop something really bad from occurring. For example, if you could lie to the Nazis about hiding Jews in your attic and save them from being killed, some people say that lie is justified because it produces a positive result. Other people would say that your moral duty is to tell the truth, because truth telling is inherently right and necessary. If your telling of the truth leads to bad consequences that is not your fault. When applied to the question of evil, we need to be clear about which ethical position we are taking. Do we believe that God could be justified in creating this world if the evil in it is necessary for the realization of a greater good, or do we believe that God could have given us something which is inherently good, even if it results in a state of affairs where evil exists?

RON. I'm not quite sure that I understand what you mean. Can you please explain that a little more? I think I understand everything except the last part about how God could give us something good which could lead to some bad or negative consequences.

JAY. Believe me, it took me awhile to figure out what was meant by that too. Basically, if God made the world good, that still doesn't mean that there could never be pain or evil in it. A major argument is that logically speaking, God could have made creatures which were fully responsible for their decisions and actions, and these actions would have serious consequences. If God made free creatures they'd have to be able to choose right or wrong. If they were to choose wrongly, of course there would be consequences. Wrong decisions, especially immoral decisions, should result in negative, painful consequences. That way we could learn to make proper decisions, and we could be free, responsible creatures whose existence and decisions really mattered in the world. According to this position, God gave us something that was very good—the ability to be moral creatures with the ability to make real decisions. This gift of responsible moral agency was a great and precious gift, and even though humans have sometimes used it for evil, the gift itself was still worth giving because of how inherently valuable such a state of existence actually is.

RON. Why wouldn't God just make us free creatures who only did what was good? Or, if he saw we were going to do something wrong, why wouldn't he just stop us?

JAY. Well, I guess we'd have to define what we mean by *free*. Who can say that God would have been better off to always intervene in this world every single time someone was going to do something wrong? Why bother making free creatures at all? How would freedom even matter in a scenario like that? What would freedom *be* in a scenario like that? The main point made by advocates of this position is that, to be meaningfully free, the individual has to be free from coercion.

RON. That's very interesting. I certainly never thought about evil from that angle before. When you think about, if choosing poorly has consequences not just for yourself but for others, it should make you more responsible with your freedom. I have this friend who was a total goofball. He spent all his time playing video games, watching sports on TV, golfing, and just being a big kid. Even when he was married he didn't reform his ways in the slightest. When he and his wife had their first baby, though, there was a big change. He was still really fun to hang out with, but you could tell he grew up in a hurry. Back when it was just young adults, he could be kind of irresponsible because it only affected him. When his daughter was born, being irresponsible would hurt both of them. So he grew up.

I could go on and on with other examples. I know someone who used to drink and drive. Not just a couple of times, but almost every weekend. He had a child too, and once that child was born, that person never drove drunk ever again. Their decisions didn't just affect them, they affected others too. My grandfather gave up smoking when my brother and I were little, because he didn't want to set a bad example for us. If it was only him, he would have smoked forever, but when your decisions affect other people, you act more responsibly.

JAY. Maybe that should be modified: we *should* act more responsibly when our decisions can hurt others. Let's just review to make sure we're on the same page here. It is logically possible that God made a good world, and part of its goodness involved the existence of genuinely free, moral creatures. In order to be free they had to have the ability to make good or bad decisions in any situation. In order for them to be responsible, their decisions had to actually matter. Their decisions would affect not only themselves, but others. Come to think of it, the Bible teaches that when humans sinned it even affected the whole creation, like the animals and nature. So it's totally within the realm of logical possibility that God's good creation could become tainted with sin, and yet that state of affairs would still be better than if he hadn't created anything at all.

RON. Yeah, that seems to make sense. None of this goes to say that this is exactly what God did, but it does demonstrate that a good, loving, powerful being and the existence of evil and suffering are not logically contradictory. Sure, somebody could say that God shouldn't have created anything at all, but that doesn't really hold water. Is it honestly certain that this world is so bad that it would be better for it never to have existed? I mean, most people, no matter how bad their life seems to be, would rather cling to life than embrace death. The vast majority of people, no matter what their circumstances, would rather be alive than dead. Despite evil, pain, and suffering, life seems to be worth living.

JAY. Another part of many theistic religions is that the future is going to get much better than the present. Think about heaven. Heaven is supposed to be the place where all pains and sorrows are vanquished. There is supposed to be a judgment day when all wrongs are made right. Even the earth is supposed to be purified from sin. Suffering is said to be necessary now, to pave the way for glory ahead. I don't pretend to understand all of that, but perhaps the present amount of evil is necessary to set up the wonders of heaven. I mean, that is possible.

RON. I wasn't sure if I should bring this up, but you sort of touched on it just now. Christian philosophers have wrestled with these issues for two thousand years, and they have demonstrated that Christianity has an internally coherent solution to the problem of evil. Even some atheist scholars admit that within Christian doctrine, the existence of evil and pain does not ruin the whole theological system.

Many Christians believe that God feels pain. At the time of Noah's Ark, the Scriptures say that God's heart was filled with pain. God's heart was grieved because he loved his creation. Maybe the more you can love, the more you can suffer. We grieve more when a close friend dies than when a stranger dies. God's capacity for love is tremendously great, and his capacity to experience emotional pain is coextensively great. Jesus is said to have suffered unimaginably more than any human has ever suffered when he died on the cross. This is mysterious to me, but if it's true it means that God has embraced and entered into suffering greater than anything we could ever experience. If God chose to create a world in which he knew he himself would suffer tremendous pain, then pain by itself can't be wrong. God is not an evil being who has set others up to suffer while he mocks at their misfortune. He himself was willing to suffer so that those who through sin caused this pain in the first place could be saved from the eternal consequences of their sins, and rewarded with eternal life in heaven. God was willing to endure ultimate suffering to free his creation.

JAY. What about hell then? Christian theology teaches that there is a perfect place called heaven, but it also teaches that there is a place of suffering called hell. What did God do to help those people?

RON. I think two main responses have been given. The first is that God doesn't need to save anyone from the consequences of their wicked decisions. If responsible, free beings choose an immoral path that leads to hell, God is under no obligation to rescue them from it. That he chose to provide a way for them to go to heaven is something that is only explainable in terms of free grace. So God didn't need to help anyone, and the fact that he did is amazing. This first response underscores that fact that God could have left all humans on their own to suffer the eternal consequences of their decisions. In love, he chose instead to provide an optional route. This also means that there is a great deal *less* suffering in the world than we ourselves actually deserve.

The second response is that God offers people the choice between heaven and hell. Sinners can be saved by trusting in Jesus Christ. They need to leave their sins behind, and ask God for forgiveness. If they don't do that, then they're making another responsible, moral decision that has great consequences. Jesus Christ suffered for sin when he was on the cross. If people want to reject the salvation that only Jesus can provide, then they literally choose to condemn themselves to hell. This just reinforces the principle that human beings are responsible to make right or wrong moral decisions. If we make the wrong ones, and we're given the opportunity to be forgiven for it, and then we reject that opportunity, well, God made us to make real, responsible, moral decisions. As we've seen, there are consequences for bad decisions, and there should be.

JAY. Okay, I can see how that fits into a Christian worldview. I found some other arguments, though, which approached the topic from a different light. Some other Christians argue that while human beings are genuinely free, God is sovereign over everything, including their moral decisions. According to this model the main point isn't that God gave man a free will, it is that God receives glory from his creation, and this is the highest good imaginable. Because we are sinful we don't recognize that God's glory is the highest good, and we even hate hearing that it is. I need to study that more carefully, but it seemed really intriguing to me. The idea that God created all things for himself more than for man somehow seems to be right. But I don't know enough about Christian theology to say which one is more accurate. Before we get too far into areas that we haven't read much about, though, I want to talk about some other areas of this topic that I was able to research.

RON. Great. Please go on.

Evil, the World, and God 55

JAY. Out of all the arguments against the existence of God from evil, I came across an argument *for* the existence of God from evil. I almost fell off my chair. All my life I've heard that a good God and evil were totally incompatible. Then I came across this argument, and it really made me think. The basic idea is that without God, there is no such thing as real evil. In fact, real evil can't exist.

RON. Once again you're going to need to explain that to me a little more fully.

JAY. I'll do my best. I can't promise that I'm going to get it all nailed down, but this is my best understanding.

The main question is: Where does evil come from in a universe where there is only matter? Was there evil at the moment when the universe came into existence? Of course not, because there was only matter. As the years went by, and matter started coming together, was there evil there? No, because matter isn't moral or immoral, it's *a*moral. It's totally morally neutral. It can't be anything else. If a comet was hurtling towards the earth, and the earth was going to be obliterated, would we say that the comet was immoral for ending all earthly life? No, because a hunk of rock isn't moral in any way.

All that's happening on earth, according to the evolutionists, is that matter is interacting with matter. There is no God. There are no spirits. There are only chemical interactions. So this chemical interacts with that chemical. Nothing moral there. The chemical composite that we call 'human' interacts with another chemical composite known as 'human.' Nothing can be moral there either. Without God there can't be any real good or evil. There is just amoral matter. If everything evolved, things are just doing what they ended up doing to survive. Morality is a dysfunctional category for explaining this reality. In this type of universe we are determined by our DNA and our environment: how we respond and the things we do are programmed by nature, not morality.

RON. I think I see. Maybe this example is similar. I've often found it absurd that in school students go from biology class where they're told that they're the result of random, accidental, purposeless forces, and then they go to a society class where they're told that they have great rights and that all humans are super valuable and precious creatures who deserve to be treated with respect and dignity. They go from "you're a nothing, existing for no purpose, and ultimately going nowhere fast in a purposeless universe" to, "you're such a special person with such special rights that you just need to realize that you can be anything you want to be." That doesn't make any sense. Then society wonders why young people act is such uncivilized ways.

JAY. That's exactly the main point of this argument. Evolution can't possibly bring you morals. It can bring you preferences, by introducing sensations that you don't like, but it can't actually bring in real right or wrong. There is simply no ground in evolutionary theory for why something *ultimately* is right or wrong.

RON. You know, I've heard that argument before, but not from people who believe in God. Many atheist philosophers have argued that there is no such thing as right or wrong because we are accidental mutations of pure matter. So the people who argue that the universe is pure matter, and yet morals are real, are trying to have their cake and eat it too. Theists say that morals are real because God is real, and many atheists say that morals aren't real because God isn't real. Secular humanists are just floating out in the middle of this crossfire. They're trying to stay in a no man's land. You can't have both, as all theists and many atheists admit.

JAY. For a while I thought that some things were just right and wrong, and that you didn't need God to make that so. Even if nothing ever existed, murder would be wrong, theoretically. But the more I thought about it, especially after our talk about design, it seemed to me to be absolutely unthinkable that these philosophical standards would exist "out there" in the abstract, and then *we'd just happen to evolve in such a way as to recognize them*! I mean, with all of the mind numbing statistics about how intricately everything in the universe needs to be balanced in order for human life to be sustained, how much more improbable is it that what evolved would be able to know timeless truth? It's just too incredible to believe. A mindless, purposeless, accidental universe that came from nothing beats the trillions and trillions to one odds of being capable of sustaining life, and then this life happens to start, happens to randomly evolve, and the final result is that we are accidentally fitted to know the deepest metaphysical and philosophical abstract, immaterial concepts of right and wrong. That could not just happen!

RON. But millions of people believe that it did, because they've already decided that there is no God. Someone once said that it takes lots of faith to be an atheist. At this point, I can see what they meant.

JAY. Listen, I don't want to cut this short, but I have to get going. I have another suggestion for you.

RON. Go ahead.

JAY. Last time we went to hear an atheist talk about why he doesn't believe in God. I think that after today we can see that his case wasn't as compelling as he thought. In order to be balanced, let's go hear a theist talk about some of the reasons they have for their faith. How does that sound?

RON. That sounds totally fine with me. Do you have any options?

JAY. Yes, I do. Easter's coming up pretty soon, and this big church in the city is hosting a seminar lecture about evidence for the resurrection of Jesus Christ. I mean, they aren't preaching about it, they're arguing for it being a real, historical event. Do you want to go?

RON. Sure thing. It'll be really interesting to hear what he has to say. I didn't know that churches bothered with anything like that—I wonder what else I don't know about them.

5

Rev. Laidler's Lecture

LAIDLER. Okay, if I can have everyone take their seat and stop chatting, we'll begin. There's a lot of ground I'd like to cover, and I tend to overestimate how much material I can get through in any given time slot, so I'm anxious to get started. If I was only talking about something ordinary I wouldn't mind so much, but in my judgment I'm talking about the most important reality in the entire universe. In fact, while at first it may seem arrogant to say, I *know* that this is the most important, and awesome, reality there is. Some of you will already agree with that, but for those of you who don't, I understand your hesitation. I used to be a militant skeptic when it came to anything that smelled like religion. But that's a tale for another time. Before we go any further, I'd like to say a short prayer.

Lord, I want to thank you for the opportunity you've given us tonight to meet together in order to talk about the resurrection of your son, Jesus Christ, from the dead. I thank you for sending your son to die on the cross so that our sins could be forgiven. I thank you tonight for the gift of eternal life that is freely given to every person who entrusts their future to Jesus, and who genuinely feels remorse for all of the wicked things they have done. I thank you that people like me who once wanted nothing to do with you can now experience an amazing relationship with you, the same God we spurned. Lord, I pray that tonight your

Spirit will work in our hearts and in our minds, to help us understand your truth, and to help us to love it. Help us we pray, for I ask it in Jesus' name, Amen.

All right, here we go. My thesis tonight is that Jesus Christ was proven to be the Son of God when he was resurrected from the dead. I bet that right now many of you think that there is absolutely no way in the world that I can really demonstrate that to you. It must be one of those blind leaps of faith. Well, yes and no. I know that I can't make you believe it. I can't take you in a time machine back two thousand years ago to watch the crucifixion and resurrection take place, but I can show you absolute, infallible proof that it happened. How? I know for sure that it happened, because the Bible, which is the Word of God, tells me so. Case closed.

Okay, okay. I can see by the look on some of your faces that not everyone is completely convinced! Stay with me, and let me explain what I mean. If the Bible is the Word of God, then everything that it contains is trustworthy. The Bible records many miracles, including the greatest miracle of all, the resurrection of Jesus Christ from the dead. So, since God's Word is truth, and it records the resurrection as a real, historical event, then the resurrection really happened. It is true.

Now, that sounds like a nasty bit of circular reasoning. Frankly, what I just said wasn't supposed to be a convincing argument, it was meant to explain to you how I know for sure that Jesus was raised from the dead. Anyone who has not been regenerated by the Holy Spirit is not likely to accept what I just said, but that doesn't mean that what I just said is wrong. So, I've given you my ultimate reason for believing in the resurrection, but now I want to present a case from evidence that I think most of us can agree on, and I want to make the argument that the evidence, considered as objectively as possible, supports my faith.

I don't want to spend too much time discussing the manuscript evidence for the accuracy of the New Testament writings, and how pristinely they have been preserved and transmitted down from the first century to the present, because even if you believe that what you read in your translations of the Bible is what the original authors wrote, that's not going to make you believe it! On the other hand, however, it is important that we understand that the majority of the original New Testament documents were written mid first century, which means that when the New Testament writings started circulating, people were still alive who had been eyewitnesses of the life of Jesus of Nazareth. This means people who had known Jesus personally were still living. Jesus had lots of friends, but he also had lots of enemies. Both hostile and friendly contemporaries of Jesus were still living when the New Testament documents were written and available.

Because Christians took their faith so seriously, and because they believed that the New Testament documents were so important, many, many copies of the original manuscripts were made. Someone would copy the Gospel of Mark and take it to Ephesus. Someone else would copy it and take it to Alexandria. Once there, scribes would make multiple copies in Scriptoriums. Manuscripts multiplied, and they were copied with unique care and precision, because the documents were treated as the inspired, breathed out words of God, given through faithful human vessels.

Since humans aren't perfect, sometimes errors would occur in copying. Occasionally, a scribe would read something which didn't make much sense to him, and so he might insert a clarifying comment in the margin. The next person to copy from this new manuscript might mistake the comment in the margin for a misplaced verse, and insert it into the body of the text. This is why some manuscript traditions have small, inconsequential variations in the biblical texts.

But since the New Testament was being independently copied all over the world, slight errors in Alexandria didn't lead to slight errors in Rome. Today, specialists known as textual critics can trace back numerous manuscript family trees, and they can determine when a textual variant appeared in the copying process. If a verse appears in AD 1200, and only in the Byzantine family of documents, we know it wasn't original. Using this process, scholars know with certainty 99.5% of the original, first century New Testament writings. The other 0.5% contains nothing theologically controversial. So, when you pick up your Bible, and you turn to the New Testament, what you are seeing are the real writings of Jesus' contemporaries, accurately passed down to you.

Okay, so what we have today in the New Testament is the same as what was originally written. That hardly does you much good if you think that what was written was either mistaken or purposefully deceptive! But it does mean that the early Christians really did teach that Jesus did many miracles, and that he was really put to death on a cross, buried in a tomb, and raised to life again after three days. Incidentally, there is no doubt that Jesus of Nazareth was a real historical person, and that he was sentenced to death by Pilate. Not only is this recorded in the New Testament, but Josephus (a Jewish historian), Tacitus (a Roman historian), and others mention this as well. Neither Josephus nor Tacitus were Christians by any sense of the imagination, although later on some of Josephus' writings were tampered with to make it seem like Josephus accepted Jesus as the Jewish Messiah. Josephus did nothing of the kind, at least in his writings, but he did record that Jesus was put to death under the reign of Pilate.

Jesus of Nazareth was an historical person who lived in the early part of the first century, and who was put to death on a Roman cross. After he had died, he was buried in a tomb. Three days later, the tomb was empty. This is an historical fact. What we need to find is the most likely explanation for the vacant tomb. Various theories have been proposed, and they are worth considering. In fact, some of the theories have denied that the tomb was empty. We'll look at them first.

One theory that denies that the tomb was empty argues that the women who went to anoint the body of Jesus got lost and went to the wrong tomb. They ran and told the disciples that the tomb was empty, and then the disciples ran to the wrong tomb as well. Of course, there was no body in the tomb. In their excitement, the disciples believed that Jesus had been resurrected, and they began to preach that this is what in fact had happened.

This theory fails because it forgets that the Romans knew where the tomb was really located, and so did the Jewish leaders. Neither the Romans nor the Jews wanted Christianity to grow, because it promoted political instability in the eyes of Rome, and religious heresy in the eyes of the Jewish leaders. So once they heard that the Christian message totally centered on Jesus being raised from the dead—and don't forget that this message was being preached just weeks after the crucifixion—they would have gone and retrieved the body. They knew where the body was. If it was still in the tomb, all that they had to do was produce the body, and Christianity would have been totally discredited. If that had happened, it would have died out immediately, and we certainly wouldn't be here talking about it! No, the tomb was empty, or Jesus' enemies would have produced the body and squelched the Christian message once and for all. They didn't do this because they couldn't.

The only theories that can be taken seriously are the theories that recognize that the tomb was empty, and then try to account for that fact. Again, the Christian explanation is certainly not the only one that has been offered. Not too long ago, a theory was seriously entertained that was known as the Swoon Theory. This theory basically asserted that Jesus did not die on the cross, he simply swooned, was mistaken for dead, buried alive, and in the cool of the tomb he was revived, got up, overpowered the guards, and made good his escape. Shortly after he showed himself to his disciples and convinced them that he had conquered death and hell. He assured them that one day their bodies would be as healthy and eternal as his!

This theory accounted for the fact that the tomb was empty. But it was pretty ludicrous. First, crucifixion was horrendous. In fact, the pain experienced was so intensive that a new word was coined to describe it: ex*cruc*iating. Nails were driven through the wrists and ankles. Jesus had been flogged, and now he was on the cross. He had lost huge amounts of blood. Perhaps he did pass out; I mean, of course many people who were crucified would have lost consciousness from time to time. So, theoretically, it would have been possible for Jesus to swoon.

Roman soldiers, however, were around suffering and death all the time. They ensured that people were really dead before they took them down from their crosses. It is highly unlikely that the Romans would have misdiagnosed a living person as being dead. If they did, it could only be because the person was as close to being dead as a human being can possibly be. But let's say that for some inexplicable reason they misdiagnosed Jesus, and buried him in the tomb. At this point Jesus, being so near to death that soldiers who saw crucifixions all the time were fooled, simply felt much better, stood up, rolled back the large, sealed stone at the entrance to the tomb, and strolled off to convince his disciples that instead of death conquering him, he had conquered it, and wasn't the worse for wear! Yeah, that's what happened.

Honestly, let's talk about reason and faith. Believing this theory is not reasonable. What's amazing is how many people jumped on the Swoon Theory bandwagon. Here's a question for you: Why were people so eager to believe something so ridiculous? Why will people believe anything except the biblical explanation? On naturalistic terms, the Swoon Theory would be totally impossible. Only people who had made up their mind that the supernatural isn't real would ever even consider it. But not only did people consider it, many people accepted it for a time. The Bible teaches that men would rather believe a lie than God's truth. It says that people won't think about God, so they have to believe anything else other than something that involves the divine. But is this reasonable, or is it based on an irrational faith in naturalism?

Moving on to some more scholarly theories for the empty tomb, we see that it is commonly argued that someone stole the body. The contenders are the Romans, the Jews, and Jesus' followers. Let's take them in that order.

First, you have the Romans. Pilate had just handed Jesus over to be crucified, to appease the Jewish leaders and to save his political skin. Pilate was a brutal man, and the Jews had just complained to Tiberius Caesar about him. In no uncertain terms Pilate was told to keep the peace, and not to get caught up in religious controversy. There is no way Pilate, who was totally looking out for number one, was going to literally risk his life in pulling this prank. He had absolutely nothing to gain, and potentially everything to lose. In fact, he ordered guards to watch the tomb to ensure that nobody tampered with the body. If the guards failed, they could lose their lives, and if the Jewish leaders were mad enough, they could force the issue to Rome and argue that the buck stopped with Pilate. Political stability in Jerusalem was a critical first century concern for Pilate, and the consequences included his own personal death. He was on thin ice with the boss in Rome, and the boss had a history of meting out harsh penalties to his underlings. There was no profit at all for the Romans which would make them inclined to steal the body.

Second, you have the Jewish leaders. They had petitioned Pilate to crucify Jesus. They considered him a dangerous rebel, and a religious troublemaker. Nothing would have pleased them more than for the death of Christ to be the death of the whole movement associated with him. If they had removed the body from the tomb they would have kept it safe and secure. Just a few weeks later, when the disciples started preaching that Jesus had been resurrected from the dead, the Jews would have publicly announced that they had actually removed the body and buried it somewhere else. It is clear from history that they never made this announcement. Incidentally, they would have made this announcement if Jesus had been buried in a mass grave. Some people, faced with the empty tomb, deny that there was any such tomb in the first place, although there's no evidence for that. They say Jesus was buried in a mass grave. But if that was the case, the Jews and the Romans would have been glad to point that out, which is something that they never did, because everybody knew Jesus wasn't buried in a mass grave. If the Jewish leaders had the body or knew where it was, there is no way in the world they would have let the Christian movement grow, when they hated it, persecuted the Christians, and all the while had the *proof* that the Christian claims were false. Neither the Romans nor the Jews stole the body.

Well, this leaves just one more interested party, the disciples. They loved Jesus, but they had fled when he was arrested and crucified. Having recovered their courage, the argument goes, the disciples organized a plot to steal the body of Jesus from the tomb, which they then went and did. It was this story, of course, which the Jewish leaders themselves used to explain the empty tomb—which, by the way, just goes to show that even Jesus' enemies acknowledged that his tomb really was empty.

Thinking up a really good reason for why the disciples wanted to risk their lives to steal the body is not all that easy to do. Let us imagine, however, that at the time stealing the body seemed like an act of homage, or some such thing, and so the disciples mustered their courage and stole the body. It would have been fairly obvious to them, I am assuming, that the corpse they were retrieving was not living. So they get the body of Jesus to wherever it is that they wanted to take it, and they grieve in private, and let's say they give him a respectful burial again. They then take stalk of their lives and say: "Let's pretend that Jesus is alive, and let's preach this message in the same city where they just killed him." This they proceed to do, for reasons that remain unclear, and at the risk of being crucified as well.

Remember at this point that they *know* what they're teaching is a lie. They know Jesus is dead, because they have the body. Yet they literally risk the same fate of crucifixion, in the same place where weeks earlier Jesus had died, and they are willing to do this for what they *know* isn't true. Listen carefully: people will die for what they mistakenly think is true, but there's no way the eleven remaining disciples were all willing to die for what they knew was a lie. Ten of them were martyred for their faith, and the last one probably died in exile on a prison island for his faith. Their lives were not outwardly improved by this lie at all. They were hated, scorned, flogged, beaten, stoned, thrown in jail, and chased around the known world for their teaching. If it was me, before I get whipped and beaten up by a crowd for what I know isn't true, I'm going to confess it. My executioner gives me the option of being stoned to death or denying that Jesus was raised from the dead. I know that I stole Jesus' body, and that he's really dead. The prospect of being killed by the throwing of stones at my body is not an attractive option. What would *you* do?

As far as I'm concerned, the only way that all of Jesus' disciples would have endured this sort of persecution and pain is if they really believed that Jesus was raised from the dead. We've already seen that the tomb was empty. How did it get that way? Well, the Bible teaches that God raised Jesus from the dead. After this his disciples endure decades of persecution, beatings, imprisonments, and ultimately die for their message. What would motivate them to do this? The only sufficient motivation was their belief that Jesus was no longer dead, but alive. Some have said that the disciples had hallucinations, but that can't be true. Crowd hallucination is different from individual. Besides that, if they just had hallucinations, Jesus' body would have still been in the tomb, and the enemies of Jesus would have been delighted to point that out. Jesus' disciples were willing to suffer the way that they did because they were convinced Jesus had died and was living again.

At one time in the history of the Western World, it could basically be assumed that people knew why Jesus died on the cross. Theologically, the Bible teaches that God created human beings without sin, but they chose to disobey God. The punishment for disobeying God was death. Jesus was the second person in the trinity, which means that he has all the attributes of deity. He willing joined his deity with sinless human nature, and he lived a perfect life. He never did anything wrong; he never sinned. Yet Jesus died on the cross, forsaken by God. Only sinners can die, because death is the just punishment for sin. How could Jesus, someone who had never sinned, die?

The answer is that when Jesus died, he was being punished for sin. Not his own sin, but the sin of his people. He willingly exchanged places with sinners, and took their punishment upon himself. God was so pleased with what Jesus did, that after Jesus had died and fully paid the penalty for sin, God raised him from the dead, to vindicate Jesus' perfections. God showed that Jesus had never displeased him. On the contrary, Jesus paid the penalty for the wicked, and this pleased God greatly. So God raised him from the dead. He was crucified and died for others, and he was raised to life because of his perfections.

This explanation allows us to understand why Jesus was resurrected from the dead, and why the resurrection is so important. It answers the question as to why Jesus should be raised from the dead in the first place. I mean, I suppose someone could think that Jesus was really resurrected, and yet not see why that's so important. If you've never thought about that before, it's important for you to see how the life, death, and resurrection of Jesus are all connected in this way.

Well, I need to wrap this up. There's much more that I'd like to say, but I don't have time. I'll be happy to talk to any of you afterwards, if you have any questions or you would like me to substantiate my points at greater length. Let me just share with you some final thoughts.

If we look at the evidence, and we look at the various theories that have been proposed to account for the historical fact of the empty tomb, the only one that makes the most sense *to someone with an open mind* is that Jesus was raised to life from the dead. A close minded person who has already ruled out the existence of God has to deny that Jesus was resurrected, of course, but that's more of a commentary on their presuppositions than it is an honest evaluation of the data at hand. I firmly believe that if none of us where Christians or Atheists, and we had to just look at the evidence without any predisposition to doubt in God's existence, we'd say that what makes the most sense is the biblical account of the resurrection. The resurrection is only rejected by those who have an anti-supernatural bias from the beginning. Why would anyone think it would be hard for a God who created the universe to raise someone from the dead?

You can still doubt the resurrection, of course, and you can still deny its validity. That's your call. But at the very least you have to recognize that there is no good reason at all for a Christian to doubt that Jesus was raised from the dead. Yes, that's accepted on the basis of faith, but on the other hand there is no historical fact, and there is definitely no empty tomb theory that discredits the resurrection. I go home tonight believing in Jesus on the basis of the work of God in my life, but also fully assured that a careful consideration of the evidence fits my faith better than any other position. This is what I would expect, given that my faith is in the truth.

Lastly, I just want to mention something else about the death and resurrection of Jesus Christ. When I said that he died for sinners, and paid the penalty for their wickedness, I meant it. But that's not the whole story. The biblical message includes the reality that you have to believe this is true in order to be saved from your sins—and not just "believe" in a superficial sense, but in the sense of committing your whole self to it. You have to believe that Jesus died on the cross to pay your penalty, and that you truly deserve death and hell for your failure to honor God in everything that you have said, thought, and done. You need to ask God to forgive you for your wickedness, and you need to trust that Jesus took your wickedness, and offers you his righteousness in its place. This great exchange was very costly. Jesus suffered and died in your place, so that you could live and spend eternity with God. To prove this, God raised Jesus from the dead. Put your trust in him today.

6

Truth and the Resurrection

JAY. Hey, Ron, anything new?

RON. Not really. I've been really thinking about some of the things that Rev. Laidler said in his presentation. Most of that was pretty new to me. I mean, I've heard preaching before about the need to accept Jesus Christ's sacrifice on the cross, and how he died in the place of sinners, but I was under the impression that you just believed that because you went to church. I had no idea that people have actually had lots of reasoned debates about the resurrection before.

JAY. I know what you mean. For me, the resurrection was always supposed to just be a religious fairy tale. It was obviously just supposed to be nonsense. I mean, you wouldn't seriously consider it any more than you would consider that the earth was flat. It was like believing in Santa Claus. When I went home and started researching, however, I found out that what the Reverend said was a pretty fair assessment of the different positions. I thought I'd probably find some killer argument that he had neglected, but I didn't. The tomb was empty, and there are only so many ways to account for it!

RON. Most of those theories had some surface possibility to them, but when the holes were pointed out, the holes were huge. If I had to construct my thoughts about it,

I'd have to say that these points were the most conclusive: One, the tomb was empty. No empty tomb, no Christianity. Two, the only people who had any motive for stealing the body and then keeping it hidden were the disciples. But, in the third place, the disciples must have believed that Jesus was really alive, or they would never have suffered and died for that message the way that they did. Fourth, this is perfectly explainable based on the existence of God and the truth of the Christian message. Fifth, no theory that denies the supernatural has even come close to accounting for the evidence. So, taking all of those considerations together, I'd have to say that unless someone is totally biased against God, the resurrection of Jesus Christ makes the most sense out of the data.

JAY. Doesn't that seem really, really hard to believe though? I mean, that God is real, that Jesus Christ was who he claimed to be, and that he was really raised from the dead? Heaven and hell both real! I can see why some people just won't accept that as the real explanation for what happened. And there are always other far out explanations that can be thrown out, like that Jesus was a cleverly disguised space alien, or that we live in a chance universe and Jesus beat all odds by experiencing something that we normally don't. But there just aren't any real reasons to believe those things, of course. And if Jesus died and came back to life then we had better accept his understanding of that event. If Jesus was a space alien he was a lying space alien—but why on earth think *that*?

RON. Honestly, I think in some ways I understand the desire to postulate anything rather than the biblical explanation for the life and resurrection of Jesus Christ. But lately I've really been asking myself *why* we're so militant in rejecting the possibility that the Christian message is true. I mean, we're supposed to be enlightened, open minded individuals. We're supposed to be rational and fair. We pride ourselves in the Western World on logical thought and reasoning. And then we're presented with a situation where the most plausible explanation involves God, and we just rule that possibility out. Why are we so resistant to the concept of the divine, if that's where the evidence seems to point? Why do we just say, without warrant, that miracles don't happen, so this account of a miracle has to be false? I mean, we say miracles don't happen, and then that becomes the reason why we reject accounts of historical miracles. But that's not based on evidence, it's based on prejudice. So when we look at the historical events surrounding the life and death of Jesus, and then the flourishing of Christianity in the first century, and the evidence seems to point towards a resurrection, why is it so easy to just shrug it off by saying miracles just don't happen?

JAY. Actually, that's what I've been struggling over too. I mean, part of this is that I don't *want* Christianity to be true. To think that God is real, that this religion is right, and that the bible is true—well, it's frightening. Going over the arguments, the preponderance of the evidence seems to point to the existence of God, but I keep thinking, *but that just can't be right*! I don't have any good reasons for that position, and in fact I can see how the faith is well supported by reason and evidence, but I just don't want that to be true and I have no idea why that is.

RON. It's interesting that the Bible does teach us that we're sinners, and that we don't want to acknowledge that God exists, in part because we don't want to recognize that we must answer to him. We don't look at the case without bias; we don't want God to be real, and we deny that he is. The only problem is that after we've done that, we still have to account for all the things in the universe, and that seems to be impossible apart from God.

JAY. And if God is real, and he did create the world, then we would expect that the evidence would point towards him. There are always qualifications, and appeals to agnosticism, but if normal standards of judgment are used, at the very least it's obvious that affirming God's existence is not irrational. In fact, the case for God's existence seems stronger than the alternatives.

RON. So where does this leave us?

JAY. Well, at the least there's no conclusive argument against the resurrection, and some reasonable arguments that support it. I can't believe I just said that, but it's true! This is the pattern we've seen over and over again. At the end of the day, reason and evidence point most clearly to God, and I just try to dismiss it uncomfortably. As the weight of the case built up, however, it got harder and harder to just dismiss. Again, my desire to easily dismiss it really caught me off guard. It just seems like I start to think that God probably exists, and then another part of me interjects, without reasoning, and tells me that there must be a better explanation. I don't know what that explanation is, but part of me desperately wants there to be one.

RON. All right, let's just say for the sake of argument that Jesus was really raised from the dead. What implications does that have for our lives today?

JAY. I'd have to say that the first thing the resurrection would mean is that Jesus is who he claimed to be, and that his teachings are true. I'm going to have to study the New Testament to find out what he taught, but I guess whatever he taught is true, since God endorsed his life by raising him from the dead. I can tell you right now that just doing that would require a massive realignment of my beliefs, priorities, and values. That's a really big implication, right from the start.

RON. I think you're right that one implication of the resurrection is that it would support Christianity's claims to represent the truth. Pluralism has told us that every religion is of equal value, and that every major religion is just as true as another, but if Jesus was raised from the dead because he was God in human form, then obviously what he said would be true. Other religions contradict Christian teachings, and that would mean that they are contradicting God, and are therefore wrong.

JAY. Wow, I can't believe how jarring that sounds in my ears! My first reaction is that no one has the right to say that their religion is better than anyone else's. But if one religion actually is true, and if God has spoken through one religion, then it does follow that that religion is correct in what it affirms and denies.

RON. Seriously, this is pretty obvious. Let's say one religion teaches that humans have a soul, and another religion teaches that humans don't have a soul. The laws of logic guarantee that both of them can't be right. When you have two contradictory positions, and there is no third position, only one is right. Humans either have a soul or they don't. Saying that both positions are equally true is nonsense.

JAY. No matter what society believes in theory, it certainly doesn't function that way, at least in practice. You say murder is wrong, but I say it's okay. Are we both right?

If one religion tells us to reject Jesus, and another tells us to put our faith in him, they're both not equally right. That type of pluralism is an inherently untenable position, when you stop and think about it. It's just more of this strange new version of tolerance that seems so popular today. I mean, we're supposed to tolerate everyone, but as soon as someone is intolerant, we don't tolerate that! We accept everyone, unless they're not as accepting as we are. We say that everyone should be included, but if someone is exclusive, we don't include them! Contemporary conceptions of tolerance are totally shot through with hypocrisy. They're self-refuting in theory, and they certainly don't work in practice. It's just amazing that pluralists don't realize that their claims for the truth of pluralism are exclusive. Since most religions see themselves as being the bearers of truth, pluralists are actually saying that every religion's self-concept is wrong—only the pluralist sees everything the way it really is. So the pluralist makes the claim that all religions are equal, but this means that the pluralist knows better than everyone in those religions who think differently. In the end, the pluralist makes himself the real truth-bearer, and demotes everyone else because of their lesser understanding. Amazing.

RON. Let's jump back to the resurrection. To my mind, the most staggering entailment to the fact of the resurrection is that it means the reason Jesus died in the first place was to pay the penalty for the sins of other people. Apart from the biblical or theological interpretation of Jesus' death, the resurrection doesn't make any sense. The only reason that Jesus, the perfect son of God, died was because he willingly chose to die for the sake of other people. If he had died for his own wrong doings, he would never have been resurrected. So the only reason Jesus was raised from the dead was because of his own perfect life, and the only reason that he died was because of our imperfect ones.

JAY. I don't totally understand the deeper theological aspects of Christianity, but this seems to be its general message: Every human being without exception has failed to be morally perfect, and God's just standard is moral perfection. There is nobody who has ever lived who could earn their way to heaven on the basis of being good enough.

Furthermore, God exists as a trinity, or three persons who have one identical essence, or nature. One of these persons took on humanity, lived a morally perfect life, and because of this life he couldn't possibly ever be punished for his sins, since he didn't have any. Yet he paid the penalty that sinners deserve, so that God's justice could be satisfied, and sinners could be forgiven. To prove that this is what happened, after he died Jesus came back to life, never to die again.

RON. Yeah, I think that's the basic message. It's like every person owes a certain amount of money for a fine. Let's just say everyone owes $100. The problem is we're all, without exception, in debt up to our eyeballs! We could never pay. But God can't simply let us off the hook. That would be unjust. Some people say that because God is loving he'll just let everything slide. But what would you think about a judge who decides to let a guilty rapist go free? What would you think if the judge said: "Oh, I'm a good and loving person, so even though you're guilty I'm just going to let you go without any hassle." There's no way you'd say the judge was either just *or* good! Same with God. His very goodness means that he won't just decide not to punish the guilty.

JAY. I think I see where this is going. We all owe a debt that we can't pay. But Jesus is morally rich, and he decides to pay our fine for us. When he does this, justice has been satisfied, because the fine has been paid, and there's no longer any legal debt that we owe. So we can be innocent in the legal sight of God.

RON. Yes, but the benefits of this standing are only realized through repentance and faith. Simply put, we have to ask for forgiveness. We have to trust in Jesus for mercy and grace. And those who have truly experienced such forgiveness will certainly start to turn their lives around for the better!

JAY. Okay, so that's the basic Christian message. I still honestly don't understand all of it, but the general contour seems relatively straight forward. I guess you get to the point where it's not so much about understanding it as it is about whether or not you're willing to accept it. I mean, you can't dance around it forever.

RON. Do you mind if I ask you a more personal question?

JAY. No, go ahead. We've talked enough so far about this kind of stuff in theoretical terms. Maybe a personal application of it is warranted.

RON. All right, then. Do you believe it? I mean, do you think that God is real? Do you think that Jesus was actually raised from the dead?

JAY. You know something, Ron? I do but I don't. Let me phrase it negatively. None of the arguments against God's existence have proven to me to be compelling. So God's existence has not been disproved at all. None of the arguments against the resurrection seem reasonable. They all basically amount to saying that the resurrection just couldn't happen, so it didn't. Hardly a reasonable position to take!

After looking at the arguments and evidence that surround the most pivotal issues in these types of discussions, I'd have to judge the case for God as being the strongest. Yet I know that my judgment in this area isn't really that important.

RON. What do you mean?

JAY. Well, I guess what I mean is that it's too pompous. *I* decide whether or not *God* is likely to exist! It's like I'm approaching the issue entirely the wrong way. If God is real, I've been trying my whole life to suppress that knowledge, and to deny that he exists. Why? Simply because I don't want to live in a universe where there's a being to whom I owe everything I am, and to whom I'll have to give an account for everything that I've done. That seriously threatens my autonomy, and my autonomy is very precious to me. I want the luxury of being able to sit around and abstractly discuss whether or not God is real. And then I can say, even if a good case is made for the fact that he does exist, that the case wasn't conclusive, so I can just keep on living my life as if I'm the center of the universe. At this point, my failure to put my trust in Jesus is far more emotional than intellectual. Frankly, I think it always has been that way, but I never really thought about it. I've hidden my pride and fears behind so called intellectual doubts. I was absolutely full of anti-God bias, before I even began to think about it.

RON. So, what are you going to do?

JAY. That's the million dollar question. I need to come to terms with what's ultimately real. If God is real, and the only way to be acceptable to him is to trust in Jesus Christ, I need to make sure that I've done that. But, on the other hand, I don't think that I can just force myself to do that. I don't think I'm ready to do that. Right now, that honestly has less to do with what I think than what I feel. I'm not ready to make that kind of commitment.

RON. Jay, I understand what you're saying. Isn't it amazing how illogical it is, though? I mean, intellectually, we think that something's true, even though we don't want it to be. Then, looking at it square in the face, we just decide not to worry about it, or not to take the next step. It's just like diet and exercise, or smoking. It's not like you really need to convince people intellectually that eating right or quitting smoking has positive health benefits, but people who know better don't do anything about it. We're a really lazy race of beings! The doctor tells you that you're a prime candidate for a heart attack unless you change your diet, work out every day, and quit smoking. Some change their lifestyle, some don't. Both intellectually acknowledge the truth, but the difference is some just don't care. They don't care if they harm their bodies. Some people just aren't willing now to make the change they need to make, in order to experience the joys of heaven for eternity. They just don't care, or they just don't think it's worth it. All I know is that winning the head and winning the heart aren't identical.

JAY. Actually, I have an aunt who is a perfect example of what you're talking about. Her immediate family pleaded with her to stop smoking. Her doctor told her about all the harmful effects. She knew smoking was terrible for her body, but she decided that giving up smoking wasn't worth it. We all thought she was nuts, and it was terrible to see her trade her life for a pack of cigarettes.

I visited her in the hospital the week before she died. You know what she said to me? She said: "Jay. I should have quit. I knew that I should. I should have quit. Now it's too late. I chose to die instead of giving up this habit. Don't throw away your life by making a mistake like this. Don't wait until it's too late to change your life for the good."

Now I'm here, and it seems like I'm faced with that kind of decision. Either give my life over to God, or decide to exchange all that God offers for my filthy habits. Funny. My stubbornness actually makes me want to hold onto the past, even though I *know* it's not worth it. I always thought I was rational. Yet here I am, and I'm seriously contemplating rejecting what I think is true, for no better reason than my aunt had for continuing to smoke. What's worse, I know that I'll regret this decision later, if I reject God.

RON. What you're saying totally fits with the way the Bible depicts the human condition. Our real problem is not intellectual, it's moral. What do we do about that?

JAY. I'm not quite sure what we can do about it. I've really enjoyed talking with you about the existence of God, and the necessity of faith. I can't make a decision right now. In many ways I wish that I could, but I can't, at least not sincerely. Would you like to get together next week, and talk about this some more?

RON. Sure, that would be fine.

JAY. I'm going to go home, and I'm going to ask God to help me to sort it all out. Part of the problem is that I want to do this on my own. I still want to be autonomous. But I don't think I can do that, not this time. If I'm going to entrust myself to God and believe that Jesus died for sinners, I'm going to need some help. So

I'm going to pray, and I'm going to ask God to help me not only reach the right conclusion, but to make the right decision on the basis of that conclusion. I don't think that I'm sufficiently strong enough to overcome my moral disinclination to accept the reality of God's claims on my life.

Then—and I can't believe I'm saying this—I'm going to read the whole New Testament. I've never done that before, so my case against Christianity wasn't exactly informed. I'm going to ask for help, and then I'm going to read. At the very least I can't think of one good reason why I shouldn't do that. What do I have to lose?

RON. Tell you what. I'll do the same thing. Let's try to read the Gospels, and then get together next week and discuss it. Maybe, if you're interested, we could go and chat with Rev. Laidler about some of this stuff.

JAY. Okay, but I want to do just one thing first.

RON. What's that?

JAY. Well, I want to study about how we actually *know* that something is true. I want to learn about how we learn, and how our minds weigh evidence and decide to accept facts. I've never thought about those kinds of things before. In all of our thinking and discussing about arguments and evidence, we've never taken the time to identify what makes a good piece of evidence in the first place, or how we can be confident that our brains function well enough to be trustworthy.

RON. Alright, then. I've never thought about those issues before. In fact, I've never even thought that those types of concerns should be treated as issues at all. But now that you mention it, we have no right to take those things for granted. Up until now we've just assumed that we can have knowledge about the way things really are, but we've never gone beyond that assumption. You've got me interested.

JAY. Good. Talk to you soon.

7

Epistemology and Facts

RON. You look a little disturbed.

JAY. Well, to be honest, I never realized that there was so much to know about *knowing*. I mean, I just totally took it for granted that my mind was reliable, that my beliefs were true, and that I always had sufficient reasons for believing what I did. Now, after having studied epistemological issues for the first time, I realize that most of my supposedly rational thinking wasn't rational at all. In fact, it's kind of frightening to consider that thinking, something we do all the time, is something that we can be so bad at, and something that we never actually think about. And perhaps the worst part of all is that all of our thinking, even our thinking about our thinking, is circular. It depends on itself, and uses itself to judge itself! If our minds aren't reliable, we obviously can't trust their conclusions—but the only way to figure out how reliable our minds are is to use them! So we just have to make the unwarranted assumption that our minds work just fine, and that they are capable of recognizing the truth.

RON. One of the things that I was really interested in researching more about was that argument we discussed earlier—the one about whether or not an evolutionist could ever know if their brain really worked. That argument intrigued me, especially because it deals with the inevitable circularity that you just pointed out. Why should we trust the processes of an accidentally formed chemical and biological system that supposedly emerged in a random, purposeless universe through the gradual accumulation of millions of blind, non-sentient mutations? The mutations were random, and nothing guided them towards intelligence. All of the chemical interactions that occurred were between non-intelligent, non-thinking pieces of matter. Why should we trust that the end result of such factors would be reliable? And how on earth did such non-sentient, non-self-conscious bits of matter come together to produce a brain capable of sentient, abstract thought? I just haven't been able to find satisfactory answers to those questions.

JAY. Yeah, that sort of thinking just reveals, again, the fact that we have to use our mutated brains to figure out if we should trust our mutated brains. It's completely circular. We pride ourselves on being logical. Why? Well, because it's logical. That's a big circle. We think we should only believe something if it's rational. Why? Well, because that's the rational thing to do. That's another big circle. And using logic or reason requires using our brains, so we have to just make the gratuitous assumption that our brains function in such a way as to recognize truth from error, and that they have such finely-tuned capabilities that they are able to reason accurately in completely abstract ways.

RON. An interesting philosophical discussion has been going on in the last few decades about whether or not—if we have evolved—it is rational to believe in rationality. The issues are pretty complicated as far as I can tell, and I'm pretty sure that I didn't get all the subtleties, but it seems that the basic question is whether or not the beliefs formed from an evolved brain can enjoy the status of being justified or warranted. Now, I guess justification and warrant are two separate properties, but that's a *really* complex issue. Basically, the main point is that for a belief to be warranted it must be formed by a mind that is working properly. What does it mean for a mind to work properly? Well, just like we discussed about the teleological argument, something works properly if it functions to achieve a particular goal or end. This, in turn, seems to require a designer, or a design plan. My car works when it moves me to where I want to go, and it can do this only when it is functioning according to the blueprints which were designed to make it mobile. The goal of its design was transportation.

JAY. I was reading about this too. What is the goal of our brains? In evolution, the goal—if that's even the right word—of everything is survival. Natural selection is just the description of what is supposed to happen in nature. The fittest survive because they reproduce, and those that reproduce are defined as the fittest. Random mutations occur, and although observed mutations are almost universally negative, the argument is that positive mutations occurred, and these helped the species in question survive better and better. Things are the way they are because they provided heightened survival value at one time.

Now, this applies to our fingers, knees, lungs and all body parts and systems. This also, then, applies to our brains. Our brains function the way that they do because their function conferred onto us some sort of survival value. The million dollar question is: What *kind* of survival value? We want to say, right away, that the survival value comes in the form of critical, analytical thinking. We survive because we are rational and logical. But why should we think that? The "design plan" of evolution is geared towards survival, not to discovering abstract truth. Perhaps if we really knew the truth we would never survive. Perhaps the world is so hopeless, so depressing, or so frightening, that if our brains really comprehended it, we'd be driven to suicide. Maybe our brains actually mutated *away* from rationality, because real rationality would be detrimental to our survival. Maybe our brains are *somewhat* rational, but they also deceive us into thinking that we're far better thinkers than we are. If I thought I was smarter than I was, I might be bolder. In a survival context, if my brain hides my weaknesses and lack of intelligence, and gives me positive self-talk, then maybe I'd think that I can figure things out. Instead of hiding in a cave and starving to death, I'd be more likely to go out and face the world, and I'd do so not because I'm as smart as I can be, but because I'm *not* as smart as I think I am!

RON. Actually, there's just no good reason not to think that we're all insane. I know people with severe mental illnesses, and they can walk down the street without getting hit by cars. They know the difference between drinking water and drinking poison. If a person thinks that they're the king of the world, they might even take extra survival precautions because they're too important to die! The ability to survive and a proper interpretation of reality are just not the same thing.

A big part of this equation is the environment. There is a long, involved history of debate about whether or not what goes on in our minds actually corresponds to the way things really are in the external world. Why should they be? How could we know, without being circular in our reasoning? I mean, we judge the outside world on the basis of our perceptions. But certainly we all know what it's like to have a perception that we misinterpreted. Why doesn't Scrooge believe his senses when the ghost of Jacob Marley appears? Well, because a little thing can affect the senses. And how can we trust our perceptions? We have to rely on our perceptions to judge their accuracy and reliability. I might know how I perceive the external world, but to say that that's the way the external world actually *is* requires operating under the unproven assumption that my perceptions and brain work accurately in the first place.

JAY. You know psychology has shown that people tend to overestimate their abilities. When people are told that they have cancer, they are more likely than is statistically rational to believe that they'll recover. How many people hear statistics, but just think "that will never happen to me"? Our minds seem to function to give us a rosier picture of life than is warranted. What else do our minds do to trick us?

RON. I'll just add one more thing about our environment. The story of naturalistic evolution is that we evolved with a certain level of eyesight, a certain range of color perception, a certain ability to judge speeds and distances, etc. This was all based on information needed for survival. Our field of perception is very limited. Look at the difference made when looking through a microscope or a telescope. Listen to the difference made when you listen through a stethoscope, or talk on a telephone for that matter. Evolution could only provide a very narrow perceptual window for survival. Why should we think that this exceptionally small perceptual window allows us to know what the world is really like? Dogs hear sounds we don't hear. Bats navigate through sonar. The perceptual, external world is different to them. In the same way that an ant could never understand the universe, why do we think that we can understand the way things really are, or that we're not just an ant colony in an analogous universe? Maybe we're just too small, too finite, and too perceptually and intellectually limited to actually comprehend reality. Perhaps we evolved with the cognitive ability to survive, which again doesn't mean that we're rational. But why think we actually know fact from fiction, or truth from error? Why trust our brains when they tell us we're smart? In fact, believing that we're rational, if we evolved, is *irrational*. There's no good reason for it.

JAY. The infinitesimally small human isn't master of truth and the universe, then. I guess it's also the case that we have to just assume that our brains end up at a mature enough place to function reliably. We know that children don't think abstractly. We've all seen teenagers with their brains still growing, and wondered how they can make some of the decisions that they do! But we just have to assume that when our brains stop growing when we're adults that they have reached a place of stability. Maybe we're more like children than we'd like to think, with brains that don't reason abstractly very well at all. Maybe we're like teenagers, and if our brains just grew for another decade we'd look back and be amazed at how dumb, short-sighted, and illogical our decisions were. In the end, we just trust that evolution did the job required to get us to a place where we can unfold the secrets of our world!

RON. So what we're saying is that the world might be a very different place than I think it is. My brain might function very differently than I think it does. My perceptions might not even be capable of perceiving the way things really are. My rational thinking might be so shot through with irrationality that I can't even recognize it. And I have to trust my brain, my perceptions, and my rational ability to even test those very things. I suppose I also have to trust my memory, since anything even a nanosecond ago is not being observed currently. Even the scientific method has to assume that our memories store information accurately, and that our memories retrieve it accurately too. We have to perceive accurately and remember accurately, but we have to trust our memories without proving that they work.

JAY. Honestly, these kinds of reflections are what drive people to skepticism. When you start working through it, you realize that you have no good reason to trust your own thinking. And, since you thought of it, you have no good reason to trust that thought either. You get to the point where to be consistent you have to be skeptical about your own skepticism. I mean, if skepticism is true you have to be skeptical about everything, including whether or not skepticism is true. And if skepticism is true, and you know it, then you can't be skeptical about everything, because you know at least one thing, namely that skepticism is in fact true. So I guess it's more a matter of principle: we just can't know for sure that whatever we think happens to be accurate, and that this is inherently self-refuting at some level. You end up intellectually paralyzed, locked in a vicious circle.

RON. The funny thing is that skeptics in philosophy don't actually live out their skepticism in real life. I was reading about a Scottish philosopher named David Hume, who has apparently had a big impact on Western philosophy in the last few centuries. He was trying to figure out how someone could actually be justified in holding to their beliefs, and how we could know for sure that our minds recognize genuine cause and effect relationships. At the end of it he basically comes to the conclusion that when we stop and think about these matters we *should* become skeptics, paralyzed from action, but in real life nature has disposed us to ignore those concerns and to go on with life. His recommendation was that when you think about these things too much you should just forget it for awhile and go spend an evening having fun with your friends. I found that pretty humorous, except that people I know act in just the same way—they start thinking about how insignificant they are in this huge universe, how they evolved from nothing, how there's no real point to life, how there's no life after death, and they get depressed. So then they just go out to a bar, go to a party, or watch a movie. They don't like what their worldview entails, so they just ignore it.

JAY. That's very interesting. I know people like that, too. But this also sets up an argument that I found really fascinating. This one was totally new to me, and I want to study it at greater length in the future. There are different facets to it, but one point was that human philosophy, when it doesn't take into account the existence of the God of the Bible, can never escape a rationality that is irrational, and an irrationality that is rational.

RON. I'm not sure I understand.

JAY. Okay, the basic thrust of this argument is that to be rational in a universe without God is irrational. As we've been talking about brains and knowledge, we've mentioned that we have no good reason to trust the deliverances of our reason. But think about that: No good *reason* to trust our *reason*. I have to use my reason to reject my reason! I'm stuck being rational so that I can affirm what is irrational. Now *that* is irrational!

Epistemology and Facts 93

So it's irrational for me to be rational, because being rational leads to irrationality. In order to be irrational, I have to use my reason. In order to be rational, I have to end up concluding that I should be irrational. There is just no way around this.

RON. But what does God have to do with this?

JAY. Well, the argument gets a little more complicated. Approached from another angle, it can be argued that unless there is perfect knowledge about everything, you can't know anything at all. This is because we understand what something is based on its relationships with other things. If I went to the middle of the jungle and found a tribe of stone age natives who had never been exposed to advanced technology before, and I gave them a pack of batteries, they would have absolutely no idea what they were. In order for them to have any understanding of what batteries are, I'd have to explain their function in terms of how batteries relate to other things. So I could say they're a source of energy, but that wouldn't make any sense unless I could demonstrate how the batteries relate to a device that runs on battery power. Frankly, most of us who use batteries all the time don't have that faintest idea what they really are or how they actually work, but we do know how to use them in relationship to other things.

RON. The main point, then, is that since everything ultimately exists in relationship to everything else, unless we know everything about everything we can never know the real relationship that things have. If we don't know all the ways everything relates, we don't really know anything about anything. I guess that means that we could be totally ignorant about the real meaning of everything. Like when people didn't know that microscopic germs caused disease—not knowing about microscopic entities caused people to totally misunderstand the nature of sickness.

JAY. Exactly. And how could we ever know for sure that ultimate reality doesn't involve a relationship that we are completely ignorant of? Unless we know everything, we can have no confidence in knowing anything for sure. It's like being forced into skepticism all over again.

RON. But, to press the point again, what does God have to do with this?

JAY. Right. God is described as being perfect in knowledge. He is all-knowing, omniscient. This means that God knows exhaustively every relationship that everything has. He completely understands the entirety of reality. His mind comprehends every detail, big or small. And then, according to the Bible, God reveals or communicates truth to his created beings. God made us so that we can understand the perfect truth that he communicates. We can accept it as truth because we trust that God knows everything. In a Christian worldview, this makes sense. In a Christian worldview, human beings can have real knowledge because God has designed them to receive truth, he knows everything perfectly, and he has revealed truth to and through his creation.

RON. Christianity, then, provides a rational justification for knowledge, and gives us a worldview where knowledge belongs and makes sense. A random, chance, accidental universe provides only reasons to be irrational, and can never give us a satisfactory accounting of why we should trust our own thoughts.

JAY. A big question emerges, though, when we think about how human beings actually live and think. We just basically assume that we can trust our brains, and that we know truth, but when we think about it, without

God there is no good reason for us to think and act like that. So why are we? Well, one answer is that God has made us to know truth, and we do come to understand some parts of creation even if we deny him. It's not that we positively don't know anything about God, it's that we do know something about him, but we suppress or ignore that knowledge because we don't want to know him. The whole thing comes back to God being the creator, humans falling into sin and rebellion, and Jesus dying on the cross in the place of the wicked, like we heard about earlier. No matter what, we can't escape the world that God made, and one penalty of this is that when we don't acknowledge him nothing in the universe can ultimately make any sense at all—but we go on trying to sort it all out anyway.

RON. I think I'm starting to see the basic argument. If, and *only* if God exists can we know anything for sure. If God doesn't exist, genuine knowledge is an impossibility. And if genuine knowledge is an impossibility, it is impossible to *know* that, so we're back into that rational/irrational problem all over again.

JAY. This is where the teeth of the argument come in: if God doesn't exist, you can't *know* that he doesn't exist, because you can't ultimately know anything at all. If you present evidence against his existence, you're actually assuming that God does exist, because you are acting as if you live in a universe where knowledge is possible, and that requires the existence of God. For any fact, any knowledge, any use of logic to be legitimate God must exist. If you don't argue against that statement, it means you accept the existence of God. If you do argue against it, once again it means that you accept the existence of God, because you have to accept his existence to justify your ability to think, reason, and to know facts in the first place.

RON. Looking back at our earlier conversations, I think there were some good arguments for the existence of God. I mean, the evidence seemed to point that way, but the arguments weren't one hundred percent convincing. They could always be doubted or debated at different points. But now in retrospect it seems that evaluating those arguments presupposes living in God's universe in the first place. If God doesn't exist, we could never reason about anything, including his very existence. Even to present evidence that seems to count *against* God's existence requires that God actually does exist in order for the evidence to be valid.

JAY. And, it should be added, that's circular reasoning. It starts with God and concludes with God. But it seems that this position is just self-conscious about what other positions depend on but deny. I mean, we've just been talking about how an ultimate criterion for reasoning is inevitably circular. I use logic because it's logical. I rely on my reason because that seems reasonable—or at least it used to, before I realized how reason drives you to be unreasonable, and how being rational drives you to irrationality.

RON. So much of this just seems to keep coming back to morals. I mean, why is this so hard to accept? Even if an intellectual case can be made for the existence of God, it still seems like there is a moral problem that keeps people from accepting it. This makes even more sense in the Christian worldview, where people do know God but deny that they do because they don't want to acknowledge his greatness. Funny, but that is totally irrational too. I mean, why would we want to deny the existence of God? Sin doesn't make any sense, but it's pretty obvious that our world does demonstrate that evil is a present reality.

JAY. Maybe a great part of it is pride. We want to be autonomous and smart. We want to make our own way, to be little gods and goddesses. You know how jealousy makes you slander and think badly about someone else? Maybe we're totally jealous of God, and we, instead of being content to be his creatures, can't stand thinking about a being who is actually greater than us. Jealousy makes us think the very worst, and also to do whatever we can to intellectually justify our negative feelings. I mean, someone is better than us at something, and we often console ourselves by thinking that they're really not that good, or that they're just lucky, or given unfair treatment, or even that they're just a lousy person. If we acknowledged that God is real we'd have to acknowledge that he is much greater than we are, and perhaps that's something that we just can't bear to do.

RON. Well, I've reached a decision. After studying about these things and talking them over with you, I've learned a lot. I also realize that there's way more to know, and way more to study. I'm not going to give up on that. But I'm going to do something that you mentioned last time: I'm going to read the Bible. I'm going to read the whole New Testament, and then go back and read the whole Old Testament. I'm not going to say that God doesn't exist until I've read every word of the Bible. And as I read I'm going to ask myself whether or not I'm rejecting something because it can't be true, or whether I'm rejecting it because *I don't want it to be true*. There's no way I can find out on my own, so I'm going to pray and ask God for help as I read. Somehow I'm starting to think that God can help me figure things out better than I can by myself. And you know, these things are too important to ignore. I'm not just going to go to a party or watch a movie. I'm going to search these things out until I find the truth.

JAY. That sounds like a plan. I'll match that. So next time we get together it's talking about the New Testament?

RON. Sure. I have to admit I'm starting to think that that will be the most interesting discussion of all!

JAY. Me too. Thanks so much for studying and challenging me to think about these issues. I've learned a ton of new stuff, and I feel like it was totally worth the effort. For once I didn't just waste my time on unimportant stuff! Seriously, thanks again. I've never read the Bible, so this is a great opportunity, and long past due. Maybe the way it works is that instead of us finding God he finds us!

RON. Could be. Somehow that would seem to make sense. Anyway, I need to get going. I need to thank you as much as you've thanked me. It has been interesting for sure, and important, like you said. The Bible—I can't believe I'm actually going to read the whole thing.

JAY. Me neither, but I want to, and I need to. So do you. I feel like I'm leaving in the morning for a strange destination, and I haven't packed anything, but I'm ready to go.

RON. Well then, I'll talk to you when you get back!

JAY. Don't forget you're going on the same trip! And who knows: Maybe when we get *there* we won't come back *here* at all—maybe we'll find something better, and we'll decide to stay.

Bibliography

Alston, William. *Beyond "Justification" Dimensions of Epistemic Evaluation*. Ithaca: Cornell University Press, 2005.

Anderson, James. "If Knowledge Then God: The Epistemological Theistic Arguments of Alvin Plantinga and Cornelius Van Til." *Calvin Theological Journal* 40, no. 1 (April 2005) 49–75.

Bahnsen, Greg. *Van Til's Apologetic: Readings & Analysis*. Phillipsburg: Presbyterian & Reformed, 1998.

———. *Always Ready: Directions for Defending the Faith*, ed. Robert Booth. Nacogdoches: Covenant Media Foundation, 1996.

Beckwith, Francis, William Lane Craig and J. P. Moreland. *To Everyone an Answer: A Case for the Christian Worldview*. Downers Grove: InterVarsity Press, 2004.

Behe, Michael, William Dembski, and Stephen Meyer. *Science and Evidence for Design in the Universe*. San Francisco: Ignatius, 2000.

Boot, Joe. *Why I Still Believe: [Hint:] It's the Only Way the World Makes Sense*. Grand Rapids: Baker Books, 2006.

Bridges, Jerry. *Is God Really in Control? Trusting God in a World of Hurt*. Colorado Springs: NavPress, 2006.

Brown, Colin. *Philosophy & The Christian Faith*. Downers Grove: InterVarsity Press, 1968.

Bruce, F. F. *The Books and the Parchments*, Third and Revised Edition. Westwood: Fleming H. Revell, 1963.

Byrne, Peter. *The Moral Interpretation of Religion*. Grand Rapids: Eerdmans, 1998.

Carson, D. A. *The Gagging of God: Christianity Confronts Pluralism*. Grand Rapids: Zondervan, 1996.

———. *How Long, O Lord? Reflections on Suffering & Evil*. Grand Rapids: Baker Books, 1990.

Clark, Kelly James. *Philosophers Who Believe: The Spiritual Journeys of 11 Leading Thinkers*. Downers Grove: InterVarsity Press, 1993.

———. *Return to Reason: A Critique of Enlightenment Evidentialism and a Defense of Reason and Belief in God*. Grand Rapids: Eerdmans, 1990.

Colson, Charles. *Chuck Colson Speaks*. Uhrichsville: Promise Press, 2000.

Cowan, Steven. *Five Views on Apologetics*. Grand Rapids: Zondervan, 2000.

Craig, William Lane and Walter Sinnott-Armstrong. *God? A Debate Between a Christian and an Atheist*. Oxford: Oxford University Press, 2004.

———. *Reasonable Faith: Christian Truth and Apologetics*. Wheaton: Crossway Books, 1994.

Dawkins, Richard. *The God Delusion*. New York: Houghton Mifflin, 2006.

———. *A Devil's Chaplain: Reflections on Hope, Lies, Science, and Love*. New York: Houghton Mifflin, 2003.

Dulles, Avery Cardinal. *A History of Apologetics*. San Francisco: Ignatius, 2005.

Feinberg, John. *The Many Faces of Evil: Theological Systems and the Problems of Evil*, Revised and Expanded Edition. Wheaton: Crossway Books, 2004.

Frame, John. *Cornelius Van Til: An Analysis of His Thought*. Phillipsburg: Presbyterian & Reformed, 1995.

———. *Apologetics to the Glory of God: An Introduction*. Phillipsburg: Presbyterian & Reformed, 1994.

———. *The Doctrine of the Knowledge of God*. Phillipsburg: Presbyterian & Reformed, 1987.

Geisler, Norman. *Christian Apologetics*. Grand Rapids: Baker Books, 1976. Reprint, Peabody: Prince Press, 2003.

Grudem, Wayne. *Systematic Theology: An Introduction to Biblical Doctrine*. Grand Rapids: Zondervan, 1994.

Harris, Sam. *Letter to a Christian Nation*. New York: Alfred Knopf, 2006.

Hick, John. *Disputed Questions in Theology and the Philosophy of Religion*. New Haven: Yale University Press, 1993.

Hoffecker, W. Andrew and Gary Scott Smith. *Building A Christian World View*, Volume 1. Phillipsburg: Presbyterian & Reformed, 1986.

Hume, David. *Principle Writings on Religion including Dialogues Concerning Natural Religion and Natural History of Religion.* Oxford World's Classics. Oxford: Oxford University Press, 1993.

Johnson, Phillip. *Darwin on Trial*, Revised and Expanded. Downers Grove: InterVarsity Press, 1993.

Kreeft, Peter. *Fundamentals of the Faith: Essays in Christian Apologetics.* San Francisco: Ignatius 1988.

Kuhn, Thomas. *The Structure of Scientific Revolutions*, Third Edition. Chicago: The University of Chicago Press, 1996.

Lewis, C. S. *Miracles.* San Francisco: HarperCollins, 2001.

———. *Mere Christianity.* London: Collins Press, 1974.

———. *The Problem of Pain.* London: Collins Press, 1957.

McDowell, Josh. *The New Evidence That Demands a Verdict.* Nashville: Thomas Nelson, 1999.

McGrath, Alister. *The Twilight of Atheism: The Rise and Fall of Disbelief in the Modern World.* New York: Galilee, 2006.

———. *The Science of God.* An Introduction to Scientific Theology. Grand Rapids: Eerdmans, 2004.

———. *Intellectuals Don't Need God & Other Modern Myths.* Grand Rapids: Zondervan, 1993.

Montgomery, John Warwick. *Evidence for Faith: Deciding the God Question.* Dallas: Probe Books, 1991.

———. *Faith Founded on Fact: Essays in Evidential Apologetics.* Newburgh: Trinity Press, 1978.

———. *Where is History Going? A Christian Response to Secular Philosophies of History.* Grand Rapids: Zondervan, 1969. Reprint, Newburgh: Trinity Press, 2001.

Moreland, J. P. and William Lane Craig. *Philosophical Foundations For a Christian Worldview.* Downers Grove: InterVarsity Press, 2003.

Morris, Henry and Gary Parker. *What is Creation Science?* El Cajon, CA: Master Books, 1987.

Nash, Ronald. *Is Jesus the Only Savior?* Grand Rapids: Zondervan, 1994.

———. *Faith & Reason: Searching for a Rational Faith.* Grand Rapids: Zondervan, 1988.

Noebel, David. *Understanding The Times: The Religious Worldviews of Our Day and the Search for Truth.* Eugene: Harvest House, 1991.

Okholm, Dennis and Timothy Phillips. *Four Views on Salvation in a Pluralistic World*. Grand Rapids: Zondervan, 1996.

Oliphint, K. Scott. *The Battle Belongs to the Lord: The Power of Scripture for Defending Our Faith*. Phillipsburg: Presbyterian & Reformed, 2003.

Peterson, Michael, et al. *Reason & Religious Belief: An Introduction to the Philosophy of Religion*, Second Edition. Oxford: Oxford University Press, 1998.

Plantinga, Alvin. *Warranted Christian Belief*. Oxford: Oxford University Press, 2000.

———. *The Analytic Theist: An Alvin Plantinga Reader*, ed. James Sennett. Grand Rapids: Eerdmans, 1998.

———. *God, Freedom, and Evil*. Grand Rapids: Eerdmans, 1977.

———. and Nicholas Wolterstorff. *Faith and Rationality: Reason and Belief in God*. Notre Dame: University of Notre Dame Press, 1983.

Ramm, Bernard. *Protestant Christian Evidences*. Chicago: Moody Press, 1953.

Reymond, Robert. *A New Systematic Theology of the Christian Faith*, Second Edition. Nashville: Thomas Nelson, 1998.

Rowe, William. *Philosophy of Religion: An Introduction*, Fourth Edition. Belmont: Thomson Wadsworth, 2007.

Rowe, William and William Wainwright. *Philosophy of Religion: Selected Readings*, Third Edition. Oxford: Oxford University Press, 1998.

Ruse, Michael. *Taking Darwin Seriously*. Amherst: Prometheus Books, 1998.

Russell, Bertrand. *Why I am Not a Christian and Other Essays on Religion and Related Subjects*. New York: Simon & Schuster, 1957.

Schaeffer, Francis. *He is There and He is not Silent*. Wheaton: Tyndale House, 1972.

Schlissel, Steven. *The Standard Bearer: A Festschrift for Greg L. Bahnsen*. Nacogdoches: Covenant Media, 2002.

Sire, James. *Naming the Elephant: Worldview as a Concept*. Downers Grove: InterVarsity Press, 2004.

———. *The Universe Next Door: A Basic Worldview Catalog*, Third Edition. Downers Grove: InterVarsity Press, 1997.

Sproul, R. C. *Defending Your Faith: An Introduction to Apologetics*. Wheaton: Crossway Books, 2003.

———. John Gerstner, and Arthur Lindsley. *Classical Apologetics: A Rational Defense of the Christian Faith and a Critique of Presuppositional Apologetics*. Grand Rapids: Zondervan, 1984.

Stackhouse, John G. Jr. *Can God Be Trusted? Faith and the Challenge of Evil*. Oxford: Oxford University Press, 1998.

Stott, John. *Basic Christianity*. Grand Rapids: Eerdmans, 1971.

Strobel, Lee. *The Case For a Creator*. Grand Rapids: Zondervan, 2004.

———. *The Case For Faith*. Grand Rapids: Zondervan, 2000.

———. *The Case For Christ*. Grand Rapids: Zondervan, 1998.

Stump, Eleonore and Michael Murray. *Philosophy of Religion: The Big Questions*. Malden: Blackwell Publishers, 1999.

Swinburne, Richard. *The Existence of God*, Second Edition. Oxford: Oxford University Press, 2004.

Templeton, Charles. *Farewell to God: My Reasons for Rejecting the Christian Faith*. Toronto: Mclelland & Stewart, 1996.

Van Til, Cornelius. *Christian Apologetics*, Second Edition, ed. William Edgar. Phillipsburg, Presbyterian & Reformed, 2003.

———. *The Defense of the Faith*. Phillipsburg: Presbyterian & Reformed, 1967.

Vanhoozer, Kevin. *Is There a Meaning in This Text? The Bible, The Reader, and the Morality of Literary Knowledge*. Grand Rapids: Zondervan, 1998.

Westphal, Merold. *Suspicion and Faith: The Religious Uses of Modern Atheism*. Grand Rapids: Eerdmans, 1993.

White, James Emery. *What is Truth? A Comparative Study of the Positions of Cornelius Van Til, Francis Schaeffer, Carl F. H. Henry, Donald Bloesch, Millard Erickson*. Nashville: Broadman & Holman, 1994.

Wilson, A. N. *God's Funeral*. New York: W. W. Norton & Company, 1999.

Wolterstorff, Nicholas. "Epistemology of Religion." In *The Blackwell Guide to Epistemology*, ed. John Greco and Ernest Sosa, 303–324. Oxford: Blackwell, 1999.

Wood, W. Jay. *Epistemology: Becoming Intellectually Virtuous*. Downers Grove: InterVarsity Press, 1998.

Zacharias, Ravi. *Jesus Among Other Gods: The Absolute Claims of the Christian Message*. Nashville: Word Publishing, 2000.

———. *Can Man Live Without God*. (Dallas: Word, 1994).

www.ingramcontent.com/pod-product-compliance
Lightning Source LLC
Chambersburg PA
CBHW070930160426
43193CB00011B/1645